# FAIR AND CERTAIN PUNISHMENT

# FAIR AND CERTAIN PUNISHMENT

*Report of*

The Twentieth Century Fund Task Force
on Criminal Sentencing

*Background paper by*
ALAN M. DERSHOWITZ

**McGraw-Hill Book Company**

New York    St. Louis    San Francisco    London    Düsseldorf
Kuala Lumpur    Mexico    Montreal    Panama    São Paulo
Sydney    Toronto    New Delhi    Singapore

**Library of Congress Cataloging in Publication Data**

Twentieth Century Fund. Task Force on Criminal Sentencing.
  Fair and certain punishment.

  Includes bibliographical references.
  1. Sentences (Criminal procedure)—United States.
I. Title.
KF9685.T9        345'.73'077        76-4776

ISBN 0-07-065623-1
ISBN 0-07-065624-X pbk.

## Contents

# Foreword

In recent years, the rising crime rate—particularly for violent crime—has made the criminal justice system the subject of heated debate. Despite considerable effort and a heavy expenditure of funds, it is clear that the various components of the criminal justice system are not working effectively or fairly. In the early 1970s, a growing awareness of the problem led the Trustees of the Fund to embark on a program of systematic research including, among other activities, the establishment of an independent Task Force to examine criminal sentencing. Criminal sentencing specifies the form in which justice shall be meted out to convicted defendants. Today it is characterized by what appear to be arbitrary disparities. Some criminals get very harsh sentences; many receive grossly different sentences for essentially equivalent crimes; and a shockingly large number go unpunished. Moreover, the decisions of the courts and of parole boards have gone largely unmonitored. These conditions have weakened the system's credibility and nurtured cynicism among defendants.

From the start of its deliberations, the Task Force, a diverse and distinguished group of authorities, agreed that the indeterminate-sentencing system that now prevails in both federal and state courts was in need of reform. The Task Force then decided to embark on the difficult and ambitious task of devising a new system, one that would serve both society and criminal offenders with greater justice and efficiency. Its plan, which embodies the certainty of punishment as a central principle, carries the promise of being much more effective and useful than the present array of capricious and irrational practices that have proved so damaging.

The Fund is grateful to the entire Task Force for its hard work and cooperation. The fact that members of the group possessed divergent philosophies concerning crime and punishment and yet were able to reach substantial agreement on an extensive change in the current system represents a real accomplishment. Special thanks are due to Edmund G. Brown, the chairman of the Task Force, for his persuasive leadership in attaining so wide a measure of agreement on the faults in criminal sentencing and how best to remedy them.

Undoubtedly, the recommendations for reform made by the Task Force are controversial. But I can personally attest that they were arrived at only after a great deal of intensive discussion and debate. Convinced that major change was needed, the Task Force had the courage to provide a blueprint for reform that it considered was in the public interest. It is my belief that this work represents a significant contribution.

M. J. Rossant, DIRECTOR
*The Twentieth Century Fund*
*January 1976*

# Members of the Task Force

# Report of the Task Force

# I/INTRODUCTION

After two decades or more of intense concern over the inadequacies of the criminal justice system, the nation still appears unable to check the rise in crime, especially violent crime. All that appears to be certain is that more of everything—more police, more courts, more prisons, more laws—will not achieve the intended objective of reform in the system of criminal justice that can ultimately lead to a lower crime rate. The increasing volume of offenses and offenders continues to overwhelm the entire system; even when improvements and efficiencies are made at one stage in the system, their chief consequence is to clog another stage. The greatest indictment of the criminal justice system in the United States is simply that it fails in providing equitable justice. Lacking credibility, it also fails in its essential purpose of protecting society by deterring criminal and violent actions.

Although the Task Force does not overlook the other serious problems that afflict the criminal justice system in the United States, we believe that perhaps the major flaw is the capricious and arbitrary nature of criminal sentencing. By failing to administer either equitable or sure punishment, the sentencing system—if anything permitting such wide latitude for the individual discretion of various authorities can be so signified—undermines the entire criminal justice structure.

The sentencing system prevailing in the United States is flawed by profound imbalance between the severity of punishment and the certainty of punishment among those convicted of crimes. (We do not deal in this report with criminals who are not apprehended or convicted of crimes.) Some convicted offenders are suffering extraordinarily harsh penalties—punishments that, to us, seem clearly in excess of the maximum sentence they deserve. Other offenders, pronounced guilty of similar crimes for which some prisoners are given extremely long sentences of incarceration, are not being punished in any real sense of the word. The irrationally disparate sentences currently imposed in the United States are not only relatively unfair but also unfair in an absolute sense: Measured against standards of fairness and effectiveness, far too many criminals receive sentences that are simply not severe enough. At the same time, far too many criminals receive sentences that are far too severe when measured against these same standards.

This Task Force believes that, unless these unfair disparities are drastically reduced, our criminal justice system will suffer increasing losses of respect and credibility among every segment of our society, from those who obey the law and those who enforce the law to those who violate the law.

*How Long Is Too Long? How Short Is Too Short?*

It is important to recognize that the concern of this Task Force is not that some sentences are too long because others are too short or that some sentences are too short because others are too long. Our criticism is that there is something basically wrong when a substantial percent of individuals convicted of armed robbery (including many repeated offenders) receive no sentence of imprisonment regardless of what other convicted armed robbers may receive. For example, only 27 percent of convicted armed robbers with substantial prior records received a prison sentence in Los Angeles County during 1970.[1] Likewise, there is something basically wrong when many persons convicted of indecent exposure (including first offenders) receive sentences of life imprisonment.[2]

Grotesque disparities are revealed in the sentences imposed for the same classes of offenders in one state as compared to another state, by different courts within the same jurisdiction, and even by individual judges meting out punishment to different offenders. Although there are few careful studies of sentencing disparity, those that have been undertaken demonstrate that unexplained and seemingly inexplicable sentencing disparity is widespread.

One recent study examined the records of felony sentences imposed by judges in one Ohio county over a two-year period. The results were a welter of different types of sentencing disparities. One judge granted probation to 26 percent of convicted offenders; another judge imposed probationary terms upon 51 percent of convicted offenders. One judge imprisoned 62 percent of convicted grand larceny defendants but only 17 percent of convicted robbery defendants. One judge imprisoned 56 percent of black defendants but only 35 percent of white defendants. These examples demonstrate three distinct types of disparity—overall disparity among the judges in the severity of sentencing, disparity within an individual judge's pattern of sentencing for different offenses, and disparity in the sentencing of black and white defendants.[3]

Here are examples from a South Carolina sample of sentencing: A female who pled guilty to voluntary manslaughter was sentenced to two years' incarceration and 4 years' probation by one judge; another judge sentenced a male defendant guilty of voluntary manslaughter to 21 years; both were first offenders. In two marijuana cases, the same judge sentenced a white youth to one year's probation and a $400 fine; a black male received a two-year sentence; again, both were first offenders.[4]

A recent study commissioned by the judges of the U.S. Court of Appeals for the Second Circuit involved 50 federal judges who were given 20 identical files drawn from actual cases and asked what sentence they would impose on each defendant.[5] In the case of a middle-aged union official convicted on several counts of extortionate credit transactions, one judge proposed a sentence of 20 years' imprisonment plus a $65,000 fine. And another judge proposed a 3-year sentence with no fine.

Questions such as "How long is too long?" and "How short is too short?" obviously are complex ones, the answers to which will depend in large part on differing views concerning the nature and purpose of punishment. But even if differences in "view" are taken into account, it is clear that, by any workable definition of disparity, the American system of sentencing is marred by unfair disparity of sentences. The same result obtains whether punishments are measured by the statute violated, by the act committed, by the offender's amenability to rehabilitation, or by comparisons with other nations. Comparative data indicate that sentences at the very high range are imposed far more frequently and are far longer in the United States than in other countries for comparable offenses and offenders. By the same token, sentences at the low range—especially sentences of no imprisonment—are also imposed for serious offenses more frequently here than in most other countries.

*A Nation of Extremes*

The fact is that we have become a nation of extremes when it comes to sentences. Because sentencing is neither fair nor effective, it harms both the individual and society. Many potential sentences are so severe that they are only rarely imposed. Even then they are imposed in a seemingly irrational manner. These realities invite abuse and threaten the credibility of the sentencing system. Credibility is weakened further when a substantial proportion of convicted defendants haphazardly escape punishment, as also often occurs.

The profound injustice of this system is keenly felt by prisoners who believe their offense was no more reprehensible than that of offenders who were perhaps placed on probation.[6] Nor are they alone in believing that "equal" defendants should be subject to equal treatment. Where equal treatment is not the rule, potential offenders are encouraged to play the odds, believing that they too will be among the large group that escapes serious sanction. Hence, the ineffectiveness of today's sentencing system in conveying the message that violations of the criminal law will be punished, thus weakening the deterrent value in prison sentences.

The inequities in sentencing are not new in the United States. They have already provoked an outcry from virtually every segment of our society. President Ford has described American sentencing provisions as "often erratic and inconsistent" and has said that the resulting "lack of uniformity is profoundly unfair and breeds disrespect for the law." As the President has also observed, "certainty of confinement" is more important than severity or length of confinement. What this statement implies is that a larger number of serious offenders should be sentenced to *some* imprisonment, even if those who are imprisoned serve *shorter* terms. This view is now widely shared by liberals and conservatives alike; it is emerging as the key element in proposals for sentencing reforms.

We recognize that structural reform of our sentencing system cannot be considered outside of the broader context of the state of the institutions that make up our criminal justice system: police, prosecutors' offices, agencies that provide defense services, courts, jails and prisons and available alternatives, and current criminal codes. A sentencing system that appears just and effective on the books may nonetheless be contributing to major injustices and inefficiencies if it is processing defendants who have been unfairly arrested or have been discriminatorily selected for prosecution or improperly convicted.

A contributing cause of the dramatic unevenness in the imposition of penalties is the fact that the sentencing system feeds convicted criminals into prisons that are often dangerously crowded and inadequately staffed—breeding grounds for further crime. Many prisons are terrible places, and, for many judges, the decision to sentence a defendant to a prison term is very difficult. Recently, the chairman of the Georgia Parole Board, in explaining why his agency had cut one year off the sentences of most inmates in that jurisdiction said,

"The situation in some prisons and jails has reached the point that simply being assigned to them constitutes punishment beyond that ordered by the court."[7]
Thoughtful consideration of sentencing problems and possible reforms cannot proceed without an initial acknowledgment of the conditions in our nation's penal institutions. It is the belief of the Task Force that structural reforms in sentencing should not lead to an increase in the already large population inhabiting the nation's prisons.* In framing our own recommendations for sentencing reform, however, we have sought to structure desirable reforms independent of the state of the prisons.

The imposition of sentence, to quote a distinguished jurist, is "probably the most critical point in the administration of criminal justice."[8] It is critical because, for the vast majority of criminal defendants, it is the only point at which a formal judicial decision is made: in some jurisdictions, over 90 percent of all criminal defendants plead guilty and thus avoid trial and appeal, as well as most pretrial proceedings. There are, of course, other important judicial decision points for defendants who plead guilty: for example, the bail decision to accept a plea to a reduced charge. But the sentencing decision—whether and for how long a defendant will be imprisoned—is by far the most critical.

We are convinced that it is possible to construct and implement a sentencing system that is both more just to individual defendants in terms of fairness and more effective in

---

*Mr. McNamara comments:*
If the introduction of our sentencing structure, which we believe to be more just and effective, should cause either an increase or a decrease in the prison population (I believe there would be a marginal increase), then the correctional system should be modified to accommodate the change. One cause for present sentencing disparities, which the Task Force has characterized as unjust, is undoubtedly the attention given to factors extraneous to the criminal behavior for which the individual is being sentenced, such as available prison space. A reasonable degree of consistency in sentencing can be achieved only if, as we recommend, the number of variables affecting the sentence is minimized.

Judge Gilmore wishes to associate himself with Mr. McNamara's comment.

terms of reducing crime than the one currently in operation. Its essential attributes must be that it is definitive in the punishments it metes out, that it distributes these punishments equitably, and that it provides appropriate punishments for the crimes committed and the circumstances.

## II/PRESENT SENTENCING STRUCTURE: INDETERMINACY AND DISCRETION

The dominant sentencing structure currently employed in the United States is based on the indeterminate sentence, so-called because it is characterized by wide separations between the legislatively authorized minimum and maximum sentences for generally defined crimes. There is an absence of articulated criteria for determining sentences. Judges are given vast discretion in sentencing offenders, and parole boards have like discretion in releasing them. These conditions have resulted from the trend over the past half-century toward "individualization of sentencing," which has had an enormous influence in shaping the penal codes of the various states.

Under current sentencing laws, state legislatures rarely decide what sentence a "typical" violator of a criminal statute should receive. Instead, they generally determine only what the minimum and maximum sentence for a given offense will be. As a consequence, attention has focused primarily on extremes. What is the *most* any armed robber should get? What is the *least* any armed robber should get? This tends to encourage unrealistic thinking about criminals. It forces the legislator to concentrate on the unusual cases, such as the mercy killer who "murders" a loved one suffering from a terminal illness, or, at the other extreme, the armed robber who forces his victims to the floor and systematically murders them. Since the imagination is virtually unlimited in coming up with extreme cases that warrant extremely different punishments, legislatures tend to set the minimum and maximum sentences at very great distances from each other. The resulting legislation tells us what the legislature thinks the appropriate penalty should be for the statistically insignificant number of situations at the extremes of the statute. It does not tell us, however, what the legislature thinks the appropriate sentence should be for the fairly typical case.

For example, many armed robberies involve most of the following elements: An unmarried male offender in his early twenties with a record for a prior armed robbery enters a small store late at night carrying a loaded pistol, escapes with several hundred dollars, and causes no harm other than the loss and fright inherent in the crime. To be sure, every such case is different in many significant respects, but most such cases are also similar in many other significant respects. Yet there is no way of knowing if a legislature, in writing an armed robbery statute that carries a maximum of 20 years and no minimum, intended an offender, convicted of this offense, to receive—all other things being roughly equal— probation, 1 year, 5 years, 10 years, or 15 years.

Contributing to this problem is the fact that legislatures tend to define crimes in very general ways. Thus, "armed robbery" may have but a single legislative definition that embraces a wide assortment of offenses, weapons, and degrees of harm plainly warranting different levels of punishments. Since the range of legislatively authorized punishment will be the same for all acts coming within that statute, the difference between the lowest and highest sentence for a given crime tends to be vast, even for relatively minor offenses. Zero to two years, for example, is not unusual for petit larceny. As the crimes become more serious, the distance increases dramatically. Zero to life is not unusual for murder. (It is rare, of course, for the court to impose "zero" imprisonment without ordering *some* formal sanction, such as a probationary term.)

Generally, there are few if any rules, standards, or guidelines, formally established through mandatory legislation, rule making, or regulation, to guide the exercise of judicial or administrative sentencing discretion. Nor are discretionary decisions on sentencing generally subject to judicial review, except in cases of clear abuse, which reviewing courts are reluctant to find. Similarly, the courts or administrative agencies generally have not articulated guidelines for sentencing typical offenders. Every judge and every parole board member has his own notion of what a fairly typical crime "deserves"—and these notions are of course disparate in the extreme.

Judicial discretion is thus very broad in most jurisdictions, with judges having considerable flexibility to tailor the sentence to the individual defendant. Indeed, the data seem to indicate that in those jurisdictions where the sentencing structure is more indeterminate, judicially imposed sentences tend to be longer. There is also some data, though far less conclusive, suggesting that sentences actually served also tend to be longer in those jurisdictions where indeterminacy is greater.¹

The area over which administrative discretion may be exercised is also very wide in most jurisdictions. Almost every state has a parole or early-release system in which an administrative agency is granted discretionary authority to release the prisoner from confinement after a specific part of his judicially imposed term or maximum has been served or at *any* time after the prisoner has begun serving his sentence. (One exception is Maine, where the legislature recently passed a law that would abolish parole entirely as of March 1976, although it would provide for substantially more "good time" than under the current sentencing structure.) The difference between the earliest possible time a prisoner becomes eligible for release and the latest possible time he may be released under a given sentence tends to be vast, especially where long sentences are imposed by the courts.

The overcrowding of prisons has exacerbated the problems created by indeterminacy of sentencing. Under the indeterminate sentence and its many variations, the basic question for the sentencing judge today tends to be "in or out." Should the defendant be sentenced to imprisonment or placed on probation? A large proportion of offenders are placed on probation simply because there is no room for them in over-crowded prisons. (Or there may be no room for them on the crowded court dockets, thus necessitating the acceptance of a plea bargain that results in probation.) Those whom the judge decides should be imprisoned are often given sentences with relatively high maximums, on the understanding that the parole board will release them earlier if the circumstances warrant it. This passing of responsibility for the length of sentence to the parole board gives the board significant flexibility to tailor, it is presumed, the length of the confinement to the prisoner's needs and performance.

It is ironic that some proponents of indeterminate sentencing originally argued that it would promote consistency of sentences, in the sense that a single releasing agency would be more likely than individual judges to sentence similarly situated criminals to roughly equivalent terms. We are not persuaded, however, that the indeterminate sentence has had this effect. Even if centralized release decision making has the potential for decreasing disparities among judicially imposed sentences, the experience with indeterminate sentencing is that it produces considerable disparities of its own.

# III/PROPOSALS FOR REFORM: FLAT-TIME AND MANDATORY MINIMUM SENTENCING

During the past decade, several important reforms to improve the fairness and effectiveness of the sentencing system within the confines of its current structure based on the indeterminate sentence have been proposed and implemented. These reforms include the establishment of sentencing institutes and sentencing panels and the appellate review of sentences.

The most prominent among these various proposals are the Model Penal Code, drawn up by the American Law Institute;[1] the Model Sentencing Act, formed by the Council of Judges of the National Council on Crime and Delinquency;[2] and the Standards Relating to Sentencing Alternatives and Procedures, proposed by the American Bar Association Project on Standards for Criminal Justice.[3] These groups have formulated general guidelines for the exercise of sentencing discretion.

Several commissions prior to this Task Force also have dealt with the issue of what criteria should guide sentencing decisions. In particular, three commissions sponsored by the federal government within the last decade have issued reports containing sentencing recommendations for implementation at both the state and federal level. These organizations included the National Commission on Reform of Federal Criminal Laws, which issued an influential report on the sentencing system in 1970.[4]

We have drawn on this entire body of research, experience, and analysis in drafting our own proposals. But while we approve of these efforts and encourage sentencing improvement of any kind, we are convinced that, without major structural overhaul, the system will continue to generate unfairly disparate sentences that bring the system into disrepute.

A major structural reform recently proposed is known as "flat-time sentencing."[5] In his 1975 Message to Congress on Crime, President Ford stated that he has asked the Attorney General to review the problem of wide disparities in sentences for essentially equivalent offenses "to ensure that the federal sentencing structure, which is now based on the indeterminate sentence, is both fair and appropriate. Among other things, it may be time to give serious study to the concept of so-called 'flat-time sentencing' in the Federal Law."

This concept—a throwback to the early nineteenth century—simply means that the legislature would define one sentence for each crime or degree of crime, that the sentence would be imposed by the judge, and that the sentence would be served in full without any discretion on the part of the parole board to order early release. Some reduction, however, would be made possible by credit for good time in prison. A number of variations on the theme of flat-time sentencing have been suggested, some with a modicum of flexibility at the judicial or administrative stages. Notwithstanding, all flat-time proposals have in common the elimination of all or most judicial and administrative discretion in sentencing and the return to the legislature of control over the determination of sentences.

Another proposal for major structural reform is called the "mandatory minimum sentence." As the term implies, this proposal would eliminate all discretion to go below a certain minimum that must be served, while retaining broad discretion to exceed that minimum up to a statutory maximum. Most proposals for mandatory minimum are limited to certain specific crimes, categories of crime, or categories of criminals.

President Ford recently proposed that incarceration be made mandatory for (1) those who commit offenses under federal jurisdiction using a dangerous weapon; (2) those who commit such serious crimes as aircraft hijacking, kidnapping, and trafficking in hard drugs; and (3) repeat offenders who commit federal crimes (with or without a weapon) that cause or could cause personal injury.[6] Mandatory minimum sentencing is embodied in the "one-year unregistered handgun" statute recently enacted in Massachusetts. Under that law, all persons convicted of possessing unregistered handguns must, without exception, be sentenced to—and must actually serve—a full year in prison. "Nobody can get you out," says the television spot that has been widely broadcast in Massachusetts.

We have seriously considered flat-time and mandatory minimum sentencing proposals. While we find many virtues in some of them, we have come to the conclusion that neither flat-time nor minimum-mandatory sentencing provides the kind of structural change that we consider essential as effective responses to the current problems of sentencing.

Flat-time sentencing goes too far in eliminating all flexibility. By requiring every single defendant convicted under the same statute to serve the identical sentence, it threatens to create a system so automatic that it may operate in practice like a poorly programmed robot. This is especially true if statutory definitions of crime remain as broad and inclusive as they are today.

These same objections apply substantially to mandatory minimum sentences for most crimes. We agree that there are certain extremely serious crimes for which imprisonment should be required without regard to the circumstances. (Our own recommendations make provision for such imprisonment.) But we reject the concept of the mandatory minimum as a general approach to sentencing. Moreover, we have concluded that a mandatory minimum sentencing structure, even if it were desirable, only addresses a small part of the critical problem of disparity and extremes in sentencing. It deals only with minimum sentences—not with the major injustices at the high end of the range.

It is our considered view that some degree of flexibility must be maintained both at the sentencing and the parole stage in order for the system to be just and effective. We have also concluded that discretion cannot be significantly reduced or controlled *without* thoroughgoing legislative (or legislatively authorized) redefinition and subcategorization of current crimes.

# IV/TASK FORCE PROPOSAL: PRESUMPTIVE SENTENCING

A sentencing system that achieves certainty of sentence with justice must avoid the evils of the present system and of the proposals to remedy it—of untrammeled discretion on the one hand and of total inflexibility on the other. The present discretion of the sentencing judge and parole board must be considerably limited and firmly guided; yet they must remain able to adapt the sentence reasonably to the particular circumstances of the crime and the peculiar characteristics of the criminal.

The Task Force proposes a system under which the legislature would retain the power to make those broad policy decisions that can be wisely and justly made about crime and do not involve the particulars of specific crimes and criminals. The sentencing judge would have some degree of guided discretion to consider and weigh those pertinent factors that cannot be wisely evaluated in the absence of the particular crime and criminal. And the parole board would have some degree of guided discretion to consider and weigh factors that were unavailable at the time of sentencing so that it could tailor its decision regarding release to the needs of the prisoner and society.

## Predictable, Specified, Limited

We call our proposal "presumptive sentencing."[1] The underlying presumption here is that a finding of guilty of committing a crime would predictably incur a particular sentence unless specific mitigating or aggravating factors are established.

The process should start with the legislature (or legislative commission or judicial body), which would break crimes down into several subcategories.* *For each subcategory of crime, we propose that the legislature, or a body it designates, adopt a presumptive sentence that should generally be imposed on typical first offenders who have committed the crime in the typical fashion.*

The legislature also would determine how much the presumptive first-offender sentence ought to be increased for each succeeding conviction according to a formula based on a predetermined percentage. The theory behind this approach is that sentences for first offenders should be relatively low but that they should increase—rather sharply—with each succeeding conviction. Thus, we have suggested a geometric progression as the appropriate increment for more serious offenses: 50 percent "enhancement" for the second armed robbery, 100 percent for the third, 200 percent for the fourth, etc. The rise would, however, be less steep for petty offenders: 10 percent for the second-time pickpocket, 20 percent for the third, 30 percent for the fourth, etc.

*The Task Force recommends that the legislature, or the body it designates, also define specific aggravating or mitigating factors, again based on frequently recurring characteristics of the crime and the criminal.* If aggravating factors outweighed the mitigating

*Mr. Silberman comments:*
Except for the proposed curtailment of the power of parole boards and prison administrators, federal, state, and local court systems need not wait for legislative action to establish a system of presumptive sentences. Courts are administrative agencies in fact if not design; as Professor Kenneth Culp Davis notes, "Earlier and more diligent use of agencies' rule-making power is a far more promising means of confining excessive discretionary power than urging legislative bodies to enact more meaningful standards." Since "power to make rules always accompanies discretionary power and need not be separately conferred," presumptive sentences for each crime, as well as the weights to be attached to prior convictions and to mitigating and aggravating circumstances, can be promulgated by courts in the form of administrative rules and guidelines. (See Kenneth Culp Davis, *Discretionary Justice* [Baton Rouge, La.: Louisiana State University Press, 1969], ch. 3, esp. pp. 56, 68.)

factors, the judge could impose a sentence that exceeded the presumptive by a specified percentage. If mitigating factors outweighed aggravating factors, the judge could impose a sentence that fell below the presumptive, again by a specified percentage. *The Task Force believes that sentencing hearings should be mandatory to establish any aggravating or mitigating circumstances and to have the sentence pronounced.* \*

In imposing sentences, judges normally consider a wide variety of factors, Some of these, such as the defendant's race, appearance, or sex, are clearly improper; others, such as whether the defendant pleaded guilty or "cooperated" with the authorities, are debatable. It is the view of the Task Force, based on its own experience and on what it has learned about the system as a whole, that different judges—acting without legislative or appellate court guidance—have different views as to whether a given factor is appropriately considered in sentencing. It is our conclusion that these issues should be openly debated, that, in situations where the factors are fairly typical and frequently recurring, the legislature (or delegated body) should decide whether these factors should be considered in sentencing.

Only in truly extraordinary and unanticipated circumstances would the judge be permitted to deviate from the presumptive sentence *beyond* the narrow range permitted by an ordinary finding of aggravating or mitigating factors. Any deviation would have to be justified in a reasoned opinion subject to a searching review on appeal. Absolute maximum or minimum sentences available to a judge in such extraordinary cases should also be established by the legislature.

---

\**Judge Gilmore comments:*
In making this recommendation, the Task Force has not, in my opinion, thoroughly considered the time demands on busy trial judges in conducting aggravation and mitigation hearings. One of our objectives is to speed the judicial process, but such hearings could considerably delay it. There are a number of devices for expediting such hearings as findings of fact by referees, stipulation of facts by both parties, and the presentation of aggravating and mitigating circumstances through probation reports and other documents made available to both the prosecution and the defense.

The parole board or releasing agency would have more limited authority than at present to release the defendant earlier than prescribed by the judicially fixed sentence. The board could decide on release, but only within a previously fixed range and on the basis of relevant information (as defined by the legislature) that was not available to the sentencing judge. The justification for early release would be to facilitate the prisoner's transition to the outside community or because of compelling medical need. As a support to prison discipline, good time should also be a reason for releasing a prisoner somewhat earlier than the date prescribed by his judicially imposed sentence. Good time would be calculated by a formula set by the legislature, for example, three days of vested good time for every month without an infraction.

In effect, we propose a complete restructuring of the functions of the releasing agency. Today, it serves primarily to determine the actual sentence to be served, which, in our view, is properly a legislative and judicial function. The vitally important function on which the releasing agency should concentrate is aiding prisoners in their difficult transition from prison routine to the outside society. The agency should help them obtain jobs, secure outpatient psychiatric treatment, get into school, reestablish their role in the family, or, if needed, enter a halfway house or other transitional institution. In order to carry out these expert functions, the releasing agency would need some power to accommodate the time of the prisoner's release to the realities of the outside world. But this power would have to be strictly limited and regulated by legislation. For example, a defendant sentenced to 24 months' imprisonment could be released after, say, 20½ months if the legislature had authorized a 15 percent reduction and if the parole board decided that such a reduction was warranted since an excellent job opportunity might not be available thereafter.

*How Different Offenses Might Be Punished*

How presumptive sentencing might work in actuality can be illustrated briefly by the ways in which several different

offenders would be punished after committing armed robbery involving the display or threatened use of a loaded gun.
We will assume that the legislature has prescribed a 2-year
presumptive sentence for a crime of this sort, with no
minimum and a 10-year maximum.

A typical first offender convicted of a typical armed robbery, with no aggravating or mitigating circumstances, would
generally receive a sentence of two years' imprisonment. But
what if the judge were to find considerable aggravating factors, such as the robbing of a blind newsstand operator or
some other particularly vulnerable victim? We will assume
that the legislature had decided that a 50 percent increase
could be imposed where aggravating factors substantially exceeded the mitigating ones. Thus, the sentence would be
three years.

Assuming that the legislature had applied a 50 percent
enhancement over the presumptive sentence for second offenses, a typical second offender convicted of the same armed
robbery would receive a sentence of three years. If the aggravating circumstances were found to outweigh mitigating
circumstances, then the sentence would be three years plus 50
percent more, or four and a half years.

But let us assume that this same offender had mercilessly
taunted and threatened his extremely vulnerable victims by
firing several shots into the air, cocking the hammer of the
pistol at their heads, and promising that the next bullet was
for them. In such circumstances, if the trial judge thought it
was warranted, he would then write a reasoned decision for a
sentence of up to eight years—beyond the addition for aggravating factors but within the legislatively prescribed
maximum—and his opinion would have to be strong enough
to overcome the legislatively prescribed presumptive sentence
of four and a half years. The extraordinary nature of a case
calling for a sentence *beyond* the established range of deviation for specified factors would have to be demonstrated by
the sentencing judge's opinion, which would be subject to
close appellate scrutiny.

There are obviously many possible variations on this concept and many possible ways of filling in the blanks. But this

illustrates in broad outline how presumptive sentencing operates.*

*Fitting the Degree of Culpability*

The development of an effective presumptive-sentencing system clearly requires careful definition of crimes and more thoughtful application of sentences to those crimes. Current sentencing laws and substantive criminal laws are often loosely organized according to outdated categorizations, e.g., "robbery," "arson," "burglary." These labels often tell us little about a particular criminal offense beyond the technical elements that define it. Although many "modern" sentencing statutes (often adaptations of the Model Penal Code) develop gradations within the broad categories of offenses, these codes rarely contain the more detailed system of punishments that we believe is necessary.[2]

The proposed new Federal Criminal Code prepared by the National Commission on Reform of Federal Laws meticulously sets out definitions of certain offenses with gradations. It also includes many significant sentencing reforms, including strict criteria for consecutive sentences, appellate review of sentences, and limitations on parole discretion.[3] But it groups all offenses into only six categories for purposes of sentencing. The need, however, is not only for detailed definitions and categorizations of crimes but also for very specific penalties for those crimes matching the relative degree of culpability and risk of harm represented by each offense. The criminal sentencing structure we propose necessarily requires more thorough lawmaking. We agree with Alexander Hamilton's observation

that a voluminous code of laws is one of the inconveniences necessarily connected with the advantage of a free government. To avoid an arbitrary discretion in the courts, it is indispensable that they should be bound down

---

*For full details of our proposals, see Appendix A, Illustrative Presumptive Sentencing Statute for Armed Robbery, and Appendix B, Illustrative List of Crimes and Presumptive Sentences, pp. 35–61.

by strict rules and precedents, which serve to define and point out their duty in every particular case that comes before them; and it will readily be conceived from the variety of controversies which grow out of the folly and wickedness of mankind, that the records of those precedents must unavoidably swell to a very considerable bulk.[4]

By "voluminous" we do not mean to suggest—nor did Hamilton intend—an unmanageable code. (A large proportion of most current criminal codes could simply be dropped, since many "crimes" are simply no longer prosecuted, nor would prosecuting them be constitutional.) Nevertheless, we believe that sentencing policies should be expressed in considerable detail. We favor *explicit* presumptive sentences for various offenses. And we believe that the factors that make a particular offense more or less serious for sentencing purposes should be clearly set out.

We are aware that in making this recommendation, we are disagreeing with the trend in recent "model" sentencing statutes—a trend that eschews detail and favors general principles. When many different kinds of crimes reflecting very different degrees of culpability and risk of harm are lumped into a very few general categories, there is an obvious need for expanded discretion. We aim at narrowing such discretion in order to create a sentencing system that is more just both to individual offenders and to society because it metes out similar punishments for similar crimes and makes punishment more certain and more credible.

In calling for new specifications, we do not suggest that the legislature separate out each crime and give it distinct statutory recognition. Such a procedure would be undesirable from the standpoint expressed above; moreover, legislatures will not, and indeed cannot, give such careful, sustained attention to creating an integrated system of criminal penalties.

*We recommend that the legislature establish a commission composed of representatives of the judiciary and other interested groups\* to undertake the drafting, establishment, and periodic review of a*

---

*Such as correctional agencies, the practicing bar, parole agencies, ex-convict groups, the police, the academy, and the general public.

*presumptive sentencing system.* In fact, vesting such bodies with responsibilities for making more careful decisions about appropriate penalties and about what circumstances are mitigating and aggravating might be a more realistic and flexible method of implementing our basic proposal and of assuring that necessary adjustments can be made without resort to the protracted process of formal legislation.

## Plea Bargaining and Simultaneous Charges

It must be admitted that presumptive sentencing is not a panacea for the sentencing problem. It leaves many issues unresolved, is capable of abuse through circumvention, and even creates certain problems of its own. For example, it does not explicitly address the issue of plea bargaining, although it was conceived with that phenomenon in mind. Bargaining in exchange for sentencing recommendations will probably be curtailed through the narrowing of judicial discretion and the elimination of the plea of guilty as a mitigating factor.* But bargaining for a reduced charge will be possible and could conceivably become more prevalent; it could also take place over mitigating and aggravating factors. ("If the defendant pleads guilty, the government will neither raise any aggravating factors nor challenge any mitigating factors.")

Our view is that plea bargaining of one kind or another will occur under any system, though it can be significantly limited if there is the will to do so. Like other structural proposals, our proposal will probably only change the locus of the bargaining and perhaps the stakes.[5] The propriety of plea bargaining—whether it is desirable to eliminate it, if this is a

---

*Mr. Silberman comments:*
It is unlikely that plea bargaining will be curtailed: under a system of presumptive sentencing, bargaining over the charge *is* bargaining over the length of the sentence, as is bargaining over mitigating and aggravating factors. But a presumptive-sentencing system, if accompanied by appropriate administrative guidelines for prosecutors, can make plea bargaining a more rational and equitable process.
Ms. Babcock wishes to associate herself with Mr. Silberman's comment.

practical possibility—will continue to be debated. But sentencing reform cannot be held in abeyance until the debate is resolved, if it ever is.

Another difficult issue is how to deal with a defendant simultaneously charged with several offenses that grew out of the same or a connected transaction or are closely related in time. Indeed, the curtailment of discretion under our proposal forces the issue to the surface, since it can no longer be dodged by the discretionary employment of concurrent sentences.

At present, a defendant who is charged with filing four false income tax returns in four consecutive years, for example, will generally receive concurrent sentences under existing laws and practices. The theory is that, once the decision to falsify is made, it would be difficult to file subsequent correct returns without arousing suspicion. Concurrent sentences are also often imposed in other quite different circumstances, as when a defendant is arrested for four armed robberies over a one-week period, though the theory here is more difficult to discern.

Under our proposal, the sentencing judge would not have untrammeled discretion to decide whether to impose consecutive or concurrent sentences; he would have to follow legislative guidelines. We have decided that a tentative approach toward possible resolution of this exceedingly complex problem would be to develop different policies concerning different kinds of situations.

A single criminal transaction could not be broken down into separate crimes for purposes of imposing consecutive sentences. Nor could the sentence for such a transaction exceed the sentence for the single most serious crime. However, a series of unrelated criminal acts or transactions could be punished by consecutive sentences. Thus, four armed robberies carried out over the period of one week could be punished by four consecutive sentences, because it would not make sense to give the criminal "free" crimes after a certain number. The best solution would probably be to devise a sophisticated system in which every additional crime in a

series carried an increment of punishment but not the full
increment of a consecutive sentence. This formula could be
applied to a continuing crime or a series of closely run crimes.
For example, all things being equal, a government official
who submits a single fraudulent bill should receive a lighter
sentence than an official who has submitted a hundred
fraudulent bills over a two-year period.

There are still other possible ways of approaching this
problem, such as imposing a top limit on consecutive offenses
for a particular type of crime. For our purposes, it is enough
to suggest that various possible solutions to the problem are
available and also to emphasize that our proposal does not
create the problem. It exists under current laws and practices
but is hidden by the exercise of judicial discretion.

*Related Recommendations*

The Task Force decided to recommend several other
improvements in sentencing that relate to presumptive sentencing but are not inherent aspects of it.

*We recommend that there should be periodic review of crime
categories; of minimum, maximum, and presumptive sentences; and
of mitigating and aggravating factors.* In our view, it is important
that legislatively determined sentences not become frozen
into permanent molds. Changing conditions, trial and error,
differing values—all require periodic rethinking of the essential components of presumptive sentencing. Accordingly, we
recommend that the sentence commission be empowered to
review the sentencing structure and make annual recommendations for changes to the legislature.

*We recommend that more imaginative approaches be taken to
sentencing by imposing punishment that mitigates the crime-breeding
effects of today's prisons.* More extensive use of weekend, vaca-
tion, and evening confinement should be considered, at least
for felons guilty of less serious crimes. More effective use
should be made of economic penalties, e.g., fines that are
measured by a percentage of income or net worth, whichever
is greater.

*We recommend the elimination of most current barriers to the employment of ex-convicts.* While sensitive to the risks of hiring persons with certain kinds of records, we are convinced that the integration of former prisoners into the job market would serve to diminish serious crime. The risks of employing ex-convicts could be spread widely through the community by means of governmental insurance. Individual entrepreneurs, especially small ones, cannot be expected to incur this risk by themselves, especially when the benefits of employing ex-convicts are likely to accrue to the society in general in the forms of reduced crime and reduced expenses associated with crime, imprisonment, and rehabilitation.

# V/STRUCTURAL REFORM AND THE LENGTH OF SENTENCES

Developing an illustrative presumptive-sentencing statute required that we decide *how long* sentences should be for which crimes and *how much* discretion should be retained in judges and parole boards. Despite disagreements concerning particular sentences for certain crimes, we are unanimous in our support for the following general quantitative changes: (1) presumptive sentences for first offenders should be set considerably lower than the prison sentences authorized today; (2) a larger number of criminals who have committed serious offenses should serve time in confinement; and (3) the area of discretion allocated to and exercised by sentencing judges and parole boards should be considerably narrowed.

In presenting our model statute,* we are merely seeking to demonstrate the kinds of decisions that must be made by legislatures under such a system. The specific numbers we have selected simply reflect the rough averaging of our individual values. Although we attempted to reach some agreement among ourselves on the "right" presumptive sentence for certain crimes, our views simply could not be merged on this issue. Some of the Task Force favored higher sentences; some of us would set sentences at a level that others felt was too low. We expect that different legislators and legislatures would have different value judgments that would yield different quantitative results from those shown in the model statute.

*See pp. 37–53.

*We urge that, in general, presumptive sentencing be accompanied by a considerable reduction in the lengths of sentences authorized by legislatures, imposed by courts, and served by prisoners. It is also our recommendation that a larger number of criminal defendants—principally those convicted of serious crime—should serve some time in prison.* If a larger number of serious criminals served prison terms that are shorter than those served today, we believe that both the justice and the effectiveness of our sentencing system would be significantly increased.

We emphasize that the structural changes inherent in presumptive sentencing are *not* designed with the specific aim of altering the current population levels of state and federal prisons. A great many persons and groups favor "decarceration," "deinstitutionalization," or significant reductions in prison populations; others favor a significant increase in the use of prisons in punishing convicted offenders, especially those convicted of crimes of violence. The Task Force does not take a position on this issue. We agree, however, that structural—as distinguished from quantitative—reform is critically needed at this time. Because we advocate prison terms of shorter average length imposed on a larger number of offenders, we assume that the adoption of such a reform would have no significant effect on the size of prison populations. In other words, the number of prisoner-days would remain constant.

The intended effect is that the vast majority of defendants with the same number of prior convictions convicted under the same section of a statute would serve sentences that clustered around the presumptive sentence for the degree of crime. The statistically small number who were outside that cluster would be truly exceptional cases. Such relative uniformity of sentences for persons of equivalent criminal records convicted of the same offense is essential to achieving fairness and effectiveness in a sentencing system. Sentences should be relatively predictable before the offense is committed. They are not predictable today. Although, for many crimes, the legislatively authorized sentence is quite high, the chance that such a penalty will be imposed, or even that *any* period of incarceration will be ordered, is often quite low.

As we noted earlier, the vagaries of sentencing—one convicted robber being sentenced to life and another being placed on probation—have seriously affected the deterrent value of criminal sanctions.[1] For many convicted offenders, there is what amounts to amnesty. And for other offenders, often undistinguishable from the first group in terms of past record, current crime, or future dangerousness, there is the injustice of the exemplary sentence. The judge, aware that most persons who commit the particular crime are not sentenced to prison, determines to make an example of this offender and thus sentences him to an unfairly long term.

Such haphazard sentencing does little to increase the deterrent impact of the criminal law, since the potential criminal is likely to calculate his potential sentence by reference to what most similarly situated offenders receive. And the sad fact today is that most criminals do not receive any or very little punishment for their crimes.

This fact presents another kind of danger, mentioned by President Ford in his speech to the California legislature. "There is a temptation," he said, "to call for a massive crackdown on crime and to advocate throwing every convicted felon in jail and throwing the key away." But this temptation must be resisted, as the President cautioned, if for no other reason than that unrealistically high penalties are counterproductive. Because juries refuse to convict, the result is often less, rather than more, imprisonment. And, as the President also pointed out in proposing mandatory sentencing for certain offenses, sentences "need not be severe. It is the certainty of confinement that is presently lacking."

It is our hope that legislatures will find acceptable the proposed trade-off between an increase in the certainty and uniformity of imprisonment for most serious crimes and a reduction in the average lengths of imprisonment authorized for typical cases. It is also our hope that legislatures will be more realistic in enacting presumptive sentences than they have been when their sole function has been to enact minimum and maximum sentences.

The Task Force recognizes that implementing its recommendations may lead to additional administrative expense at a time when the fiscal health of many cities and states is in question. But to avoid that cost means incurring another serious kind of cost—loss of respect for the law enforcement system as it is perceived by both offenders and citizens in general. Injustice and unfairness will continue, and so will a continual dilution of the deterrent effect of the criminal justice system. And that amounts to a bad bargain.

# Appendixes to the Report

# A/ILLUSTRATIVE PRESUMPTIVE-SENTENCING STATUTE FOR ARMED ROBBERY

We present in this appendix an illustration of how an armed robbery statute might be drafted in the context of a presumptive-sentencing system. This model has three degrees of applicability in the design of statutes for other crimes.

First are provisions, such as the definitions of the crimes and the minimum, maximum, and presumptive sentences for each, that would have to be drafted anew for each crime.

Second are provisions, such as the power of the releasing agency, that would be equally applicable to all crimes and would not require drafting anew. In an actual statute, such general provisions would appear but once and would be written in general terms to cover all crimes.

Third are those provisions that could be written either in general terms applicable to all crimes or in specific terms applicable to particular crimes or categories of crime. For example, the list of aggravating or mitigating factors, as we have drafted them, would be generally applicable to many crimes. But it would be possible, of course, to tailor these factors more precisely to individual crimes or categories of crime.

A like option would exist for the increment for each prior offense. The same figure (25 percent) could be used generally for all cases. Or different bases (say, 10 percent for less serious crimes and 50 percent for more serious crimes) could be used. Solely for illustrative purposes and not as an inherent part of our proposal, we have used different bases for each crime but have applied a geometric progression for each additional offense.

## Breaking Down the Crime

*Armed robbery in the first degree* is the forcible taking of property from the person of another by the use of a loaded gun, where the offender discharges the gun with intent to injure or kill another person.

*Armed robbery in the second degree* is the forcible taking of property from the person of another by the use of a deadly weapon other than a loaded gun, where the offender uses that weapon with intent to seriously injure or kill another person.

*Armed robbery in the third degree* is the forcible taking of property from the person of another by the use of a loaded gun, where the offender discharges the gun under circumstances in which the likelihood of personal injury is high.

*Armed robbery in the fourth degree* is the forcible taking of property from the person of another by the display of or threat to use a loaded gun.

*Armed robbery in the fifth degree* is the forcible taking of property from the person of another by the use or attempted use of a deadly weapon other than a loaded gun under circumstances in which the likelihood of personal injury is high.

Some may believe that this description of armed robbery in the fifth degree is more serious than the conduct set out for the fourth degree and that, as a result, the two should be reversed. This judgment would be a reflection of how significant the involvement of a gun—merely its display to the victim—should be in an assessment of the seriousness of an offense. Different legislatures or courts might well reach different conclusions on the issue of whether fourth and fifth degree armed robbery are properly ranked in this statute.

*Armed robbery in the sixth degree* is the forcible taking of property from the person of another by the display of or threat to use a deadly weapon other than a loaded gun. This subcategorization is merely illustrative and obviously could be refined and improved upon. The intention here is to emphasize the considerable differences between armed robbery where a loaded gun is discharged and armed robbery where a knife or unloaded gun is merely displayed. The point we are trying to make is that these differences can be considered by the legislature in advance, without reference to the facts of particular crimes or the backgrounds of particular criminals.

*Presumptive, Minimum, and Maximum Sentences for Armed Robbery*

It must be emphasized that the figures that follow are merely averages intended to illustrate the range of appropriate sentences. They should not be construed as recommendations of the Task Force. The only consensus we have reached on length of sentences is that they should be considerably shorter than they are today.

For *armed robbery in the first degree,* the presumptive sentence for offenders with no prior criminal record shall be imprisonment for 5 years; the minimum sentence shall be imprisonment for 3 years; the maximum, imprisonment for 12 years.

For *armed robbery in the second degree,* the presumptive sentence for offenders with no prior criminal record shall be imprisonment for 4 years; the minimum sentence shall be imprisonment for 2 years; the maximum sentence, imprisonment for 10 years.

For *armed robbery in the third degree,* the presumptive sentence for offenders with no prior criminal record shall be imprisonment for 3 years; the minimum sentence shall be imprisonment for 1 year; the maximum sentence, for 8 years.

For *armed robbery in the fourth degree,* the presumptive sentence for offenders with no prior criminal record shall be imprisonment for 2 years; the minimum sentence shall be imprisonment for 6 months; the maximum sentence, imprisonment for 6 years.

For *armed robbery in the fifth degree,* the presumptive sentence for offenders with no prior criminal record shall be imprisonment for 1 year; the minimum sentence shall be imprisonment for 6 months; the maximum sentence, imprisonment for 5 years.

For *armed robbery in the sixth degree,* the presumptive sentence for offenders with no prior criminal record shall be imprisonment for 6 months; the minimum sentence shall be probation for 1 year; the maximum sentence, imprisonment for 4 years.

*Presumptive Sentences for Multiple Offenders*

The presumptive sentence for all defendants who have been lawfully convicted of one or more felonies during the five years prior to the commission of the armed robbery for which they now face sentence shall be calculated in the following way.

For *one prior conviction*, the presumptive sentence shall be the presumptive sentence for the degree of armed robbery for which the defendant now faces sentence *plus* 50 percent of the presumptive sentence either for the felony for which he was previously convicted or for the degree of armed robbery for which he now stands convicted, whichever is less.

Here are two illustrations:

The presumptive sentence for a defendant presently facing sentence for armed robbery in the fourth degree who was convicted once before, during the preceding five years, of armed robbery in the fourth degree could be three years. The calculation is two years as the presumptive sentence for armed robbery in the fourth degree and 50 percent of that, or one year.

The presumptive sentence for a defendant presently facing sentence for armed robbery in the third degree who was convicted once before, during the preceding five years, of

armed robbery in the fourth degree would be four years.
Here the calculation is three years as the presumptive sentence for armed robbery in the third degree and 50 percent of the presumptive sentence for armed robbery in the fourth degree, or one year, which is less than 50 percent of the presumptive sentence for armed robbery in the third degree.

For *two prior convictions*, the presumptive sentence shall be the presumptive sentence for the degree of armed robbery for which the defendant now faces sentence *plus* 100 percent of the presumptive sentence for either the felony for which he was previously convicted or for the degree of armed robbery for which he now stands convicted, whichever is less.

In calculating here the presumptive sentence for two prior convictions, the same process is involved as for one prior conviction except that (1) the increment is 100 percent rather than 50 percent; (2) one of the convictions may have occurred more than five years before the crime in question, as long as at least one of the convictions did occur within the five-year period; and (3) the first conviction occurred within five years prior to the second conviction. In other words, any period of five years without a felony conviction erases all prior convictions.

For *three prior convictions*, the increment shall be 200 percent; for *four prior convictions*, 400 percent; for *five prior convictions*, 800 percent, until the maximum sentence is reached.

The theory behind this approach is that sentences for first offenders should be relatively low but that they should increase—rather sharply—with each prior conviction; thus, we have suggested a geometric progression as the appropriate increment. Neither the percentage we have selected nor the rate of increase are inherent in our presumptive-sentencing proposal. Nor is our suggestion for erasure of felony convictions after five conviction-free years. These, like all the rest of our figures, are merely intended to be suggestive and illustrative.

Theoretically, the penalty for repeated offenses could be escalated beyond the maximum sentence authorized by the legislature. Such a system would, however, pose serious constitutional questions as well as problems of justice. A defendant who has repeatedly been convicted of a relatively petty offense, such as shoplifting goods of a value of less than $100, could well be subject to life imprisonment if penalties for recidivists were escalated and a legislative maximum imposed no ceiling on the possible sentence.

## Aggravating Factors Considered by Judges Today

In an effort to construct a list of aggravating circumstances, we began with a rather inclusive catalogue of factors that are probably considered—by at least some judges—in imposing sentences. Some of these are clearly improper, such as the defendant's race, appearance, and sex. Others are debatable, such as whether the defendant pleaded guilty or cooperated with the authorities. Our experience suggests that different judges—acting without legislative or appellate court guidance—have different views as to whether a given factor is appropriately considered in sentencing. It is our conclusion that these issues should be openly debated, that in situations where the factors are fairly typical and frequently recurring, the legislature should decide whether they should be considered in sentencing.

Below is the full list we compiled of aggravating circumstances that are probably given consideration by judges today. It is followed by our own selection of those we believe to be appropriate.

*Aggravating circumstances surrounding the crime itself:* large number of victims, particularly vulnerable victim (e.g., blind old newsstand operator, etc.), desire for personal profit, pleasure-seeking ("thrills"), leadership of the criminal enterprise, unwillingness to make restitution, large sum of money (or value of goods) stolen, victim treated particularly cruelly during course of offense.

*Aggravating circumstances relating to the criminal's background:* on probation or parole at time of crime, organized crime connections, large number of prior offenses, large number of prior incarcerations, prior violations of probation and/or parole, defaults on prior court appearances, social class.

*Aggravating circumstances relating to the criminal's conduct at and about the time of the trial:* perjury at trial, insistence on going to trial, refusal to cooperate with authorities, contemptuous behavior at trial, refusal to testify against codefendants, refusal to cooperate in making future cases (testifying before grand jury, etc.), high sentence recommendation by district attorney, unsympathetic recommendation by probation department, lack of contrition.

*Aggravating circumstances relating to the criminal's future dangerousness:* other similar crimes committed *after* this one (while on bail), continuing drug problem, refusal to participate in therapy, relative youth of offender, race, need to deter others in community from engaging in similar conduct, desire to incapacitate particular offender for protracted period.

After considerable debate among members of the Task Force about which of these to recommend, we could only agree on those few listed below. To our minds, this disagreement demonstrates most dramatically the necessity for having open legislative debate about the mitigating and aggravating factors that are appropriately considered by a sentencing judge. There are undoubtedly many that we simply failed to think of and that, had we thought of them, might well have been included in the consensus. Again, however, our list is merely illustrative and suggestive. Our point is that the legislature should—through open debate—decide which among the typical recurring factors should and should not be considered by the sentencing judge.

*"Aggravating" and "Mitigating" Factors Legislatively Defined*

*Aggravating factors*  None of the factors listed below is explicitly related to a predictive judgment about a defendant's future dangerousness. Thus, all the factors set out here would enhance a defendant's punishment because of the particular circumstances of the crime he had already committed; none of the factors would serve to lengthen the term of imprisonment because of a crime he might commit in the future. Although the Task Force has made no specific recommendations concerning the validity of the role of predictions of dangerousness in sentencing, this issue has been recently under intensified scrutiny.*

1. The defendant was the leader of the criminal enterprise.
2. The crime involved several perpetrators.
3. The crime involved several victims.
4. The victim or victims were particularly vulnerable.
5. The victim or victims were treated with particular cruelty during the perpetration of the crime.
6. The degree of physical harm inflicted on the victim or victims was particularly great.
7. The amounts of money or property taken were considerable.
8. The defendant, though able to make restitution, has refused to do so.
9. The defendant had no pressing need for the money taken; he was motivated by thrills or by the desire for luxuries.
10. The defendant has threatened witness or has a history of violence against witnesses.

*Mitigating factors*   The following may be considered by the sentencing judge as mitigating factors.

1. The defendant played a minor role in the crime.
2. The defendant committed the crime under some degree of duress, coercion, threat, or complusion in-

*See, for example, N. Morris, *The Future of Imprisonment* (1974), pp. 66–73; A. von Hirsch, "Prediction of Criminal Conduct and Preventive Confinement of Convicted Persons," *Buffalo Law Review*, 21 (1972):717; A. Dershowitz, "Preventive Confinement: A Conceptual Framework for Constitutional Analysis," *Texas Law Review*, 51 (1974):1277.

sufficient to constitute a complete defense but which significantly affected his conduct.
3. The defendant exercised extreme caution in carrying out the crime.
4. The victim or victims provoked the crime to a significant degree by their conduct.
5. The defendant believed he had a claim or a right to the property.
6. The defendant was motivated by a desire to provide necessities for his family or himself.
7. The defendant was suffering from a mental or physical condition that significantly reduced his culpability for the offense.
8. The defendant, because of his youth or old age, lacked substantial judgment in committing the crime.
9. The amounts of money or property taken were deliberately very small and no harm was done or gratuitously threatened against the victim or victims.
10. The defendant, though technically guilty of the crime, committed the offense under such unusual circumstances that it is unlikely that a sustained intent to violate the law motivated his conduct.

*Range of Judicial Discretion in Considering Aggravating and Mitigating Factors*

The sentencing judge shall conduct a sentence hearing for purposes of establishing mitigating or aggravating factors set forth by the defense and the prosecution.

Although the Task Force did not agree upon particular "standards of proof" for establishing aggravating and mitigating factors, the various possibilities are apparent. It could be required that aggravating circumstances be established by "clear and convincing evidence" or even "beyond a reasonable doubt." A "preponderance of the evidence" might suffice to establish a mitigating factor. Or the standard of proof could be the same for factors in either category.

After such a hearing, the trial judge shall determine whether each of the aggravating or mitigating circumstances on the legislature's list has been established. He may also decide that a given factor not listed above constitutes an aggravating or mitigating circumstance. If he so decides, he must write a reasoned opinion indicating why such factor is appropriately considered in sentencing.

If the number of mitigating factors substantially exceeds the number of aggravating factors, the sentencing judge may reduce the presumptive sentence for the particular offender (presumptive sentence plus increment for prior convictions) by up to 50 percent. If the number of aggravating factors substantially exceeds the number of mitigating factors, the sentencing judge may increase the presumptive sentence for the particular offender by 50 percent.*

For example, the presumptive sentence for a defendant who is convicted of robbery in the fourth degree and who has two prior convictions for the same offense would be three years (two years plus 50 percent of two years). If the mitigating factors substantially exceed the aggravating factors, the trial judge may reduce the sentence to no more than one and a half years (three years minus one and a half years). If the aggravating factors substantially exceed the mitigating factors, he may raise the sentence to no more than four and a half years (three years plus one and a half years). Thus, in the ordinary case, the effective sentencing range for armed robbery in the fourth degree with two prior identical offenses would be one and a half to four and a half years.

In any case, where the mathematical calculation permits the sentencing judge to impose a sentence of six months or less, he may instead impose a sentence of probation of up to one year, but he must write a reasoned opinion explaining the reasons why no sentence of imprisonment was imposed.

---

*Mr. von Hirsch comments:
The presumptive-sentencing structure should also recognize that some mitigating or aggravating factors may be more important or serious than others and therefore could be assigned different weights.
Judge Gilmore wishes to be associated with Mr. von Hirsch's statement.

Here is an example: A defendant with no prior record who is convicted of robbery in the sixth degree would receive a presumptive sentence of six months. If the mitigating factors clearly outweighed the aggravating factors, the sentencing judge would have the power to reduce that to three months. In our view, he should also have the discretion—when good reasons can be given—for substituting a probationary sentence for such a crime.

In cases where imprisonment of one year or less is imposed, the sentencing judge may order that such sentence or any portion thereof may be served on a staggered basis, e.g., during weekends, holidays, evenings.

*The Handling of Extreme and Special Cases*

In extreme and special cases, where extraordinary aggravating conditions exist, the sentencing judge may impose any sentence up to the maximum authorized by the legislature for the offense. If the judge imposes a sentence in excess of 50 percent above the presumptive sentence for the particular offender, he must justify that sentence in writing by refering to overwhelming considerations which demonstrate that such a sentence is both necessary and just. On appeal,* the trial court's reasons for imposing a sentence outside the range of the presumptive sentence plus the increase for aggravating factors shall be subject to strict review and must overcome the presumption in favor of a sentence within the normal range of deviation.

By way of illustration, take the case of a defendant convicted of armed robbery in the first degree who was previously convicted of murder. His presumptive sentence would be seven and a half years. But the evidence reveals that after he had robbed the storeowner, he gratuitously shot at him at point blank range; his prior conviction, for which he served a

---

*\*Mr. T. Williams comments:*
Appeal, in these cases, should be mandatory since many convicted defendants often remain ignorant of their rights and avenues of appeal.

long sentence, was also for a gratuitous murder committed after an armed robbery. In this case, a maximum sentence of twelve years seems justified; yet it is in excess of that permitted under the presumptive sentence. In this case, the judge may decide that the "presumption" has been overcome and may impose the maximum sentence. The presumption in favor of the presumptive sentence continues to operate, however, through the appellate process. (These figures are solely illustrative.)

We are aware that this example is a bit strained, since the defendant could be convicted of attempted murder, a crime that would carry a higher presumptive sentence, but there are cases where no other crime could be charged and where a sentence in excess of the presumptive range would be warranted. This kind of limited flexibility for the truly rare and special case is required, we believe, but it must be reserved for only such cases, and the strong burden must be on those who would deviate from the presumption.

In extreme and special cases where extraordinary mitigating factors exist, the sentencing judge may impose any sentence down to the minimum authorized by the legislature for the offense. The same procedure and burden as applies in the previous section shall apply here as well.

In extreme and special cases where any imprisonment or the imprisonment required by the statute would cause serious medical problems, the sentencing judge may impose another punishment in lieu of imprisonment. Such punishment shall, to the degree feasible, be equivalent in impact to the imprisonment called for by the statute.

Even more rigid procedural requirements than those we have suggested could be imposed to make it more and more difficult to impose a term in excess of the presumptive sentence in anything but the truly extraordinarily aggravated case. The sentencing judge's opinion might have to demonstrate the necessity and justice of the enhanced punishment "beyond a reasonable doubt." A unanimous vote for affirmance might be required from the reviewing court.

*Concurrent Versus Consecutive Sentences*

As observed in the text of the Task Force report, difficulties arise under presumptive sentencing in dealing with several offenses that grow out of the same or a connected transaction or that are closely related in time. Our proposal by no means creates this issue, but rather forces it to the surface because it is no longer hidden by the discretionary employment of concurrent sentences. We believe that several different approaches or principles are required in coping with this very difficult problem.

The first principle is that a single criminal transaction cannot be broken down into separate crimes for purposes of imposing consecutive sentences, nor can the sentence for such a transaction exceed the sentence for the single most serious crime. Thus, a defendant convicted for a single armed robbery cannot receive consecutive sentences for such component crimes as possession of a weapon, assault with a deadly weapon, burglary, larceny, and trespassing; his maximum exposure would be for the sentence (presumptive plus the increment, except in extraordinary cases) prescribed for armed robbery (or whatever the single most serious crime was).

The second principle is that a series of unrelated criminal acts or transactions can be punished by consecutive sentences, as in the example of four armed robberies carried out over the period of one week. We are aware that, although this is permitted under current law, it is not generally done today and could result in unrealistically long sentences. But we see no reasonable alternative other than to devise a sophisticated system in which every additional crime in a series carries an increment of punishment, but not the full increment of a consecutive sentence. And perhaps this may prove to be the best solution.

The third principle is that a continuing crime or a series

of closely run crimes should also be punished by an incremental sentencing. The example used is that of a government official who submits a single fraudulent bill versus an official who has submitted a hundred fraudulent bills over a two-year period. It would be unconscionable to punish the latter a hundred times more harshly than the former. Some legislative formula making the latter practice a *different* and more serious crime with gradually increasing penalties for each new violation makes more sense than adding an entire consecutive sentence for every fraudulent bill.

A top limit could be imposed, of course, on consecutive offenses for a particular type of crime. For example, no one convicted of larceny, regardless of how many transactions were involved, could receive a sentence in excess of ten years. Or no sentence in excess of a given maximum (say, 25 years) could be imposed regardless of the type or number of crimes charged. However, this raises the related problem of whether the government must try a defendant at the same time for *all* crimes it intends to charge him with. The Task Force takes no position on this, except as it relates to sentencing.

*Role of the Releasing Agency*

The judicially imposed sentence shall be served in full with two exceptions, the first based on good time, the second on factors not available to the sentencing judge.

For each calendar month in which the prisoner has not been found to have committed any substantial violation of any lawful rule of the institution, he shall irrevocably earn three days of good time. This means that a "model" prisoner could cut approximately 10 percent off his judicially imposed sentence by complying with all rules. It is important that the amount of good time be set in advance, since legislatures and judges will often base their sentencing decisions on a realistic assumption of the amount of time a prisoner will actually serve. Very large amounts of permissible good time, therefore, may become self-defeating, since the sentence will be set higher with the anticipated "discount" already calculated.

The releasing agency shall be authorized to reduce the

judicially imposed sentence by 15 percent (in addition to the good time) on the basis of factors not available to the sentencing judge that bear on the prisoner's transition to the outside community. Thus, a model prisoner could have a total of 25 percent cut off his judicially imposed sentence, but the 15 percent beyond the 10 percent good time would have to be justified by reference to information unavailable to the sentencing judge and bearing directly on his transitional needs, such as the availability of a job or educational opportunity.

We have not dealt extensively with the need for due process guarantees in parole proceedings because, in our proposed structure, the parole board has significantly less sentencing power; therefore, not so much is at stake as is in the current system. Similarly, we have not made detailed recommendations concerning permissible parole conditions or the scope of a parole officer's surveillance powers because the period a releasee would serve on parole is relatively short in our system.

*Procedural Safeguards*

The Task Force's general approach to the issue of procedural safeguards in sentencing is that more extensive safeguards are required where more discretion is permitted and where more is at stake in the sentencing decision. In other words, where the decision of a judge may determine whether a defendant is sentenced to life imprisonment or probation, more extensive safeguards are required than where the judge's decision is limited to whether the sentence may be three, four, or five years. The same is true of decisions made by release agencies. Where a parole board has discretion to release a given prisoner after 1 year or after 20 years, then procedural safeguards should be more extensive than where the parole board's power is limited to releasing the prisoner after 85 percent of his sentence has been served.

The current law presents a combination of evils—extremely broad discretion to impose widely disparate sentences coupled with minimal procedural safeguards. Under our proposal, the discretion of both sentencing judges and parole boards would be significantly narrowed; the effective range of their decisions would be substantially reduced in the vast majority of cases. Thus, the need for extensive safeguards would not be nearly so compelling as it is under existing laws and practices. Nevertheless, we have concluded that some additional safeguards are required. Again, it must be emphasized that no one of the safeguards, though strongly recommended, is inherent to our presumptive-sentencing proposal. With this general background in mind, we suggest the following general procedural safeguards:

1. As mentioned earlier, a due process sentencing hearing at which the defendant is given an opportunity to present mitigating factors and challenge aggravating factors and at which the government is permitted to present aggravating factors and challenge mitigating factors
2. Appellate review of sentences, especially of those sentences that deviate from the presumptive sentence*

Although sentencing-reform proposals generally favor appellate review of sentences, there is no clear agreement on the issues of whether both the state and the defendant should be accorded a right to appeal and whether the reviewing court should be vested with powers to raise, as well as lower, sentences.

Some feel that, in order to assure evenhandedness by the sentencing courts, excessive leniency as well as excessive harshness should be subject to correction by the reviewing

*Mr. McNamara comments:
I believe that the suggestion to mandate appellate review of sentencing merits far more consideration due to the probable impact that it will have on the judicial process. The likely proliferation of appeals could well exacerbate problems caused by the present heavy court workload. Alternative measures should be explored for ensuring that a presumptive-sentencing structure is adhered to. It would indeed be ironic if the Task Force recommendations led to an increase in the court delays that we identified as a contributing factor to the present ineffectiveness of the American criminal justice process.

court. Similarly, some argue that giving the appellate court powers only to reduce sentences will encourage a substantial number of frivolous appeals by wishful defendants. On the other hand, the mere possibility that the reviewing court may increase a sentence may discourage valid appeals by defendants who are fearful that an exercising of their right of appeal may be "punished" by the court. Some commentators believe that an appellate court's increasing of a criminal sentence may be illegal under the principle of *North Carolina v. Pearce,* 395 U.S. 711 (1969).

This Task Force has not made a specific recommendation on this issue. Because our proposal relies upon presumptive sentences and aggravating and mitigating factors that are established by legislative or administrative bodies, we place considerably less emphasis on the role of judicial review than do those reform proposals that look to the appellate courts to create a "common law of sentencing."

# B/ILLUSTRATIVE LIST OF CRIMES
# AND PRESUMPTIVE SENTENCES

The Task Force has outlined how several common crimes might be handled under a system of presumptive sentencing. The crimes we have selected are burglary, homicide, aggravated assault, rape, the "fencing" and receiving of stolen goods, bribery, and larceny. The purpose here is not to draft detailed model sentencing statutes for each of the crimes. Rather, it is to illustrate an approximate range of presumptive sentences for a variety of offenses.* It is our view that, before it can be decided what an appropriate sentence would be for a given crime, the range of sentences for other crimes should be considered as well.

*Mr. McNamara comments:*

The Task Force's recommendation that shorter sentences be given but that they actually be served is a badly needed reform to introduce some credibility into the present chaos. But, even though the figures in Appendixes A and B are averages and are not recommendations of the Task Force, I am concerned that some are so low that they will cause our general recommendation for lower sentences to be misunderstood and shunned by the legislative officials we hope to influence. The shorter range of sentences we present, in actuality, may be fairly close to the prison time now served for these crimes. However, we must not forget that the public is generally unaware of this fact and will perceive the recommended revisions as a radical change. Legislators will probably avoid reforms that could easily be misunderstood by the public as "softness toward crime." In particular, the sentencing range for violent recidivists seems too low. Furthermore, the ten-year sentence for premeditated murder is surely going to be controversial. The recent enactment of legislation reimposing the death penalty in several states is a clear indication that this figure will cause much debate and could cause the whole report to be misunderstood. I believe that the public is generally unaware that the average time served for those convicted of first-degree murder is within this range. Indeed, the public would be most opposed to this practice, if it were aware of

Although we have not included minimum sentences for the illustrative crimes selected, we are prepared to recommend that imprisonment be made mandatory for all crimes of violence involving the display or use of a loaded gun. We must emphasize, however, that this recommendation is not an inherent part of our presumptive-sentencing proposal.

It should also be noted that the number of months or years set out in the following model statutes have not been endorsed by this Task Force or by its individual members as the "correct" presumptive sentences. The figures represent only a rough averaging of our quite varied views. A complete drafting job would, of course, require a listing of minimum and maximum sentences for each crime, but, since the focus of this report is on the presumptive sentence, we have limited our catalogue to such sentences.

*Burglary*

The presumptive sentence for a breaking and entering of the dwelling of another in the nighttime with the intent to commit a felony

---

it, especially in the more brutal murder cases. For example, § 4 under the suggested homicide-sentencing approach designates a four-year sentence that could be applied for the actions that led to the tragic death of eleven people in the LaGuardia airport bombing case of December 1975. Could we in good conscience support this type of sentence?

The sentencing range for fencing, receiving stolen goods, and larceny also appears to be unrealistically low in terms of obtaining public or legislative support. Few merchants or business leaders are likely to accept these ranges as valid deterrents, and those groups are capable and likely to influence legislators against a sentencing scheme that carries such low penalties. Finally, the most disturbing aspect of these recommendations is the suggestion that probation be extended upon a second shoplifting conviction under $100. I firmly believe that the penalty for recidivism while on probation for any offense should never entail extending probation. If probation failed as a deterrent, it represents the most illogical, wishful thinking to suppose that more of it will be successful. Such measures can only increase disrespect for the process by offenders, victims, and the public. In summary, I think the sentencing scheme is theoretically sound and with some rather slight increases in the sentencing ranges could be presented as a viable legislative package.

Judge Gilmore wishes to associate himself with Mr. McNamara's comment.

1. When committed while the lawful occupants were at home and when the defendant brandishes a weapon in their presence: 24 months.
2. When committed while the lawful occupants were at home but under circumstances such that the defendant, although armed with a weapon, did not confront them or brandish a weapon in their presence: 18 months. (This type of burglary could be further refined to separate our different types of unoccupied dwellings—seasonal homes, for example, as opposed to homes left unoccupied for an evening, etc.)
3. When committed in an unoccupied dwelling by a defendant armed with a weapon: 12 months.
4. When committed in an unoccupied dwelling by an unarmed defendant: 6 months.
5. When committed in a clearly abandoned dwelling: probation for 6 months.

*Homicide*

The presumptive sentence for

1. The premeditated, deliberate killing of another: 10 years. (Though this may seem an extremely low sentence, even when the possible 50 percent increase for aggravating factors is considered, it is congruent with the average term of imprisonment actually served by persons currently convicted of murder in the first degree.)
2. The intentional killing of another under circumstances in which the defendant was not initially the physical agressor or subject to serious provocation: 5 years.
3. The intentional killing of another during the course of a felony by any of the participants in the felony who did not actually commit the murder: the sum of the presumptive sentence for the felony plus the presumptive sentence for either (a) manslaughter or (b) second-degree homicide, whichever is the proper

measure of the defendant's culpability in the particular felony-murder. (In essence, this provision recommends the abolition of the felony-murder rule; it advocates, instead, that such offenders receive consecutive sentences for the constituent parts of the crime.)

4. An unintentional killing of another resulting from reckless conduct under circumstances in which the risk of death was extremely high and that risk was known ot the defendant: 4 years.

5. An unintentional killing of another resulting from gross negligence that the defendant did not contemplate as posing a risk of harm to another: probation for 1 year.

## Aggravated Assult

The presumptive sentence for

1. A premeditated assault in which the defendant was the initial aggressor and in which serious, permanent physical harm was intended for the victim and accomplished: 6 years
2. An assault in which the defendant was the initial aggressor but in which the defendant did not plan the assault or intend serious, permanent physical harm: 2 years
3. An assault in which the defendant was not the initial aggressor but in which the defendant substantially exceeded that degree of force which would be justified as self-defense: 6 months.

## Rape

The presumptive sentence for

1. Any person who commits a rape and also assaults the victim and causes bodily injury: 6 years

2. Any person who commits a rape but causes the victim no additional serious bodily harm: 3 years

3. Any person who commits an unaggravated rape upon another who has previously been a sexual partner: 6 months.

Aggravating factors that, if found by the sentencing court, may increase the sentence shall include: (1) the fact that the victim was under 15 or over 70 years of age and (2) the fact that the victim was held captive by the offender for a substantial period of time (over two hours).

*Fencing*

The presumptive sentence for any person found guilty of fencing stolen property: one year. (This "one category" crime reflects a judgment that *all* fences are professionals and that the offense is simply not subject to rational gradation on the basis of degrees of seriousness.)

*Receiving Stolen Goods*

Any person found guilty of receiving stolen goods on the basis of evidence showing that he has occasionally (one or two instances) purchased goods knowing them to have been stolen shall be sentenced to a probationary term of 3 months. The presumptive sentence, upon a second conviction: 1 month's imprisonment.

*Bribery*

The presumptive sentence for

1. A government officer holding a position of very high trust (an elected or appointed official serving as governor, mayor, judge) who solicits and/or accepts something of value as consideration for a particular agreed-upon action in his official capacity: 3 years.

2. A government officer holding a position of very high trust who solicits and/or receives something of value from one seeking illegally to influence official acts under such circumstances that the officer understands the illicit purpose of the transaction but enters into no specific agreement with the giver concerning what particular acts by the officer will "earn" the payment: 1 year.

3. An elected government officer holding a position as a legislator who engages in the conduct described in § 1: 2 years.

4. An elected government officer holding a position as a legislator who engages in the conduct described in § 2: 6 months.

5. Any government official or employee holding a position other than those described in § 1 but who engages in the conduct described in § 1: 1 year.

6. Any government official or employee holding a position other than that described in §§ 1–4 who engages in the conduct described in § 2: permanent suspension from government employment.

7. Any person who makes the gifts or payments described in §§ 1–5: one-half the term applicable to the receiver of such gift or payment.

8. Any person who makes the gift or payment described in § 6: 3 months' probation. A second conviction for the same offense: a sentence of 3 months.

A mitigating factor for persons charged under §§ 7–8 would be the fact that the defendant was in danger of being improperly deprived of property or position as a result of threats from the government official or employee. If found by the court, this would decrease the presumptive sentence.

*Larceny*

The presumptive sentence for

1. Any person who with threats of force or violence but

without actual resort to force or violence takes the property of another: 24 months.

2. Any person who by trickery or fraud takes the property of another of a value of over $500: 6 months.

3. Any person who is employed by an institution and who embezzles the goods or funds from that institution of a value less than $1,000: 3 to 6 months.

4. Any person who shoplifts from a retail store goods of a value less than $100: probation for 1 year. A second conviction for the same offense: a 1-year probationary term to run from and after the prior probationary term with such second conviction not being grounds for the revocation of the prior probation. A third conviction: a sentence of 1 month in prison.

5. Any person who under claim of right, and without threats of force or violence, takes property owned by an institution: a probationary term of 6 months.

# NOTES

## Chapter I

[1]P. W. Greenwood et al., *Prosecution of Adult Felony Defendants in Los Angeles County: A Policy Perspective* (Santa Monica, Calif.: The Rand Corporation, 1973), p. 110.

[2]See, for example, the California case of *In re Lynch* (8 Cal. 3d 410, 1972) discussed in the background paper.

[3]L. Cargan and M. Coates, "The Indeterminate Sentence and Judicial Bias," *Crime and Delinquency*, 20 (1974):144.

[4]L. J. Toliver et al., *Sentencing and the Law and Order Syndrome in South Carolina* (St. Paul, Minn.: West Publishing Co., 1974).

[5]A. Partridge and W. Eldridge, eds., *The Second Circuit Sentencing Study: A Report to the Judges of the Second Circuit* (Washington, D. C.: The Federal Judicial Center, 1974).

[6]See, for example, Citizens' Inquiry on Parole and Criminal Justice, *Prisons without Walls: Report on New York Parole* (1975), summarized in *Criminal Law Bulletin*, 11 (1975):273; *Official Report of the New York State Special Commission on Attica* (1972); and V. Taylor, "The Correctional Institution as a Rehabilitation Center—A Former Inmate's View," *Villanova Law Review*, 16 (1971):1077.

[7]The Georgia Parole Board granted an across-the-board commutation to all prisoners serving sentences of over two years with the exception of inmates who (1) are serving sentences for crimes of violence, (2) are serving sentences for the sale of narcotics, or (3) have pending appeals or other court proceedings.

[8]M. Frankel, *Criminal Sentencing: Law without Order* (New York: Hill and Wang, 1972), p. vii.

## Chapter II

[1]See, for example, S. Rubin, "Long Prison and the Form of Sentence," *National Probation and Parole Association Journal*, 2 (1956):337, 344–347; P. Tappan, "Sentencing under the Model Penal Code," *Law and Contemporary*

*Problems,* 23 (1958):528, 531; N. Morris, *The Future of Imprisonment* (Chicago: University of Chicago Press, 1974), p. 48.

## Chapter III

[1] American Law Institute, *Model Penal Code, Proposed Official Draft* (Philadelphia: American Law Institute, 1972).
[2] Council of Judges of the National Council on Crime and Delinquency, *Model Sentencing Act,* 2d. ed. (1972). See also Board of Directors, National Council on Crime and Delinquency, "The Nondangerous Offender Should Not Be Imprisoned: A Policy Statement," *Crime and Delinquency,* 19 (1973):449, reprinted in *Crime and Delinquency,* 21 (1975): 315, with several critical articles.
[3] American Bar Association Project on Standards for Criminal Justice, *Standards Relating to Sentencing Alternatives and Procedures* (Chicago: American Bar Association, 1971). See also *Standards Relating to Probation* (1970), *Standards Relating to Appellate Review of Sentences* (1968), and *Standards Relating to Pleas of Guilty* (1968).
[4] President's Commission on Law Enforcement and Administration of Justice, *The Challenge of Crime in a Free Society* (1967), *Task Force Report: The Courts* (1967), *Task Force Report: Corrections* (1968); National Commission on Reform of Federal Criminal Laws, *Study Draft of a New Federal Criminal Code, Part C: The Sentencing System* (1970); National Advisory Commission on Criminal Justice Standards and Goals, *A National Strategy to Reduce Crime* (1973), *Task Force Report: Corrections* (1973).
[5] See D. Fogel, *We Are the Living Proof: The Justice Model for Corrections* (Cincinnati: W. H. Anderson Co., 1975).
[6] President Ford's proposal would limit the exceptions to mandatory imprisonment to persons (1) under 18, (2) mentally impaired, (3) under substantial duress, or (4) who were minor participants in another's crime.

## Chapter IV

[1] For an argument on other grounds in favor of presumptive sentences, see A. von Hirsch, *Doing Justice: The Choice of Punishments,* Report of the Committee for the Study of Incarceration (New York: Hill and Wang, 1976), chap. XII.
[2] See Council of Judges of the National Council on Crime and Delinquency, op. cit.; American Law Institute, op. cit.; National Commission on Reform of Federal Criminal Laws, op. cit.
[3] See the comparative discussion, L. B. Schwartz, "Shortcomings of the McClellan Bill," § 1 (analyzed and compared with the Brown Commission recommendations), *Criminal Law Reporter,* 17 (1975):3203–3205.
[4] *The Federalist Papers,* No. 78.
[5] See, for example, R. Moley, *Politics and Criminal Prosecution* (New York: Minton, Balch and Co., 1929), pp. 44–45. The author charts the close relationship between decreases in one form of discretionary disposal of cases and increases in other methods toward that same end.

## Chapter V

[1]Our view that the certainty of punishment is more important as a deterrent than the severity of punishment has been consistently supported by recent studies. See M. R. Geerken and W. R. Gove, "Deterrence: Some Theoretical Considerations," *Law and Society Review,* 9 (1975):497, 500–502.

# Background Paper

*By Alan M. Dershowitz*

# *I/The Purposes and Mechanisms of the Criminal Sentence*

The sentence of imprisonment, though employed sporadically throughout history, has become the dominant form of criminal sentence only during the last two centuries. Despite its relative recency, and despite some current calls for its abolition, the sentence of imprisonment is likely to retain its central role in the criminal justice system for the foreseeable future.

The primary objective of the criminal sentence, especially the sentence of imprisonment, is to reduce the frequency and/or severity of the harms caused by criminal acts and omissions.[1] The pursuit of this objective may emphasize any or all of three considerations: *isolating* the convicted criminal from the noncriminal population, which will then be protected from any harm he might do; *punishing* the convicted prisoner so that he—and others contemplating crime—will be deterred from doing harm by the prospect of the painful response he may incur if convicted; and *rehabilitating* the convicted criminal so that his desire or need to commit future crimes will be diminished.

## ISOLATION

Isolation has been used throughout history against all manner of "dangerous" beings, human as well as animal. During the period of removal, the isolated criminal cannot—with some obvious exceptions—commit crimes against the rest of us.[2] Isolation may take the form of imprisonment, banishment, exile, deportation, hospitalization, house arrest, or enforced enlistment in the military. In order to operate effectively, the removal of the convicted offender need not be accompanied by any pain or inconvenience other than that inherent in the isolation itself. Theoretically, if uncontaminated by considerations of punishment and rehabilitation, the purpose of isolation could be served by installing the convict at an escape-proof resort, equipped with every amenity, including family members and friends who chose to join the convicted person in his isolation. Suffering, inconvenience, and loss of freedom, money, and status generally accompany isolation. But, at least in theory, they are unintended side effects. As Chief Justice—then Judge—Burger euphemistically put it, in the context of indeterminate confinement for an exhibitionist: "We need not assess 'fault' on the lewd actor; but we must be able to remove him from public areas—gently but firmly—in order to protect the public. . . ."[3]

The use of isolation in criminal sentencing involves the assumption that a significant number of the persons to be isolated would, if permitted to remain in the general population, commit crimes against that population. It is impossible to determine the number and the degree of seriousness of the crimes that would be committed by those currently isolated.[4] And even if this number could be determined, it might not represent a significant percentage of the total amount of serious crime in a given jurisdiction.[5]

It is difficult to judge the effectiveness of isolation as a technique of crime prevention without controlled experiments, which—for understandable reasons—society is reluctant to authorize.[6] Obviously, isolation prevents some serious crimes, but random isolation of the same percentage of the population might also prevent some serious crime, since any randomly selected population is likely to include some individuals who would commit serious crimes. The larger the group and the longer the period of isolation, the greater would be the number of crimes prevented. Of course, the population of convicted criminals currently sentenced to prison includes a significantly larger percentage of individuals who will commit crimes in the future than does a randomly selected population. But whether the population of those currently sentenced to prison includes the largest feasible percentage of such individuals is not certain. Putting aside the question of preventively confining dangerous persons who have not "yet" been convicted of serious crime,[7] the population of those currently selected for imprisonment *from the pool of individuals convicted of serious crimes* does not necessarily include the largest feasible percentage of future crime committers.

Of course, a variety of considerations properly limit our ability and willingness to confine only the population with the highest percentage of future serious crime committers. For example, relatively few of those convicted of premeditated murder, compared to those convicted of armed robbery, are likely to commit future crimes. But the seriousness of the crime also influences the determination as to whether and for how long defendants should be imprisoned. To the extent to which that concern focuses on protecting society at large, the nature of past conviction is not relevant except insofar as it confers "jurisdiction" on a particular system[8] and insofar as it is predictive of future serious crime. Indeed, several forms of isolation that have been, and are currently, employed by our society purport to focus exclusively on prevention of future harms: mental hospitalization and quarantine are but two examples.

Isolation in prison is intended, in most cases, not only as quarantine but also as punishment.

## PUNISHMENT

The purpose of punishment is to produce a "hurt." The purpose of this hurt is to discourage future crimes. This mechanism of crime control is older than recorded history.

Despite frequent protestations to the contrary, it can be demonstrated that some punishments deter some crimes by some people.[9] Were it not for parking tickets, there would be more double parking; conversely, as the cost of using a parking lot approaches the cost of a parking ticket, illegal parking also tends to increase. Of course, 10-year sentences do not necessarily deter more manslaughters than 8-year sentences. It is almost impossible to demonstrate the precise effectiveness of a given punishment on a given crime. The most extensive studies of "deterrence" have been directed at the death penalty, particularly in the United States. But these studies, the methodology of which has been widely criticized, have not produced convincing evidence that the death penalty deters potential murderers (or prevents particular murders, such as those of law enforcement officials) more effectively than does a long prison sentence.[10]

The severity of the penalty may be less important than such factors as the certainty and promptness of its infliction on all who commit the crime; the degree to which potential crime committers are aware of the penalty, its certainty, and its promptness; and the relationship between the "benefits" of the crime and the "costs" of punishment to potential crime committers.

Of the three major approaches to the criminal sentence, only punishment is designed to serve purposes in addition to reducing the frequency and/or severity of criminal harms. Criminal punishment has always had important symbolic and other nonutilitarian goals.

Immanuel Kant argued that, even if no possible advantage can be found in punishing a given criminal, the punishment must nonetheless be imposed.[11] To illustrate the categorical nature of this imperative, he constructed his famous example:

> Even if a Civil Society resolved to dissolve itself with the consent of all its members—as might be supposed in the case of a People inhabiting an island resolving to separate and scatter themselves throughout the whole world—the last Murderer lying in the prison ought to be executed before the resolution was carried out. This ought to be done in order that every one may realize the desert of his deeds, and that bloodguiltiness may not remain upon the people; for otherwise they might all be regarded as participators in the murder as a public violation of Justice.

Most contemporary Western thinkers reject the Kantian notion of punishment. Many also reject the extreme opposite view—espoused by the Italian positivists during the last quarter of the seventeenth century[12]—that punishment and justice should have nothing to do with criminal sentences; that considerations of public safety and social defense should be the sole determinants of whether and for how long a convicted criminal should be confined. The difficult question to be faced by concerned citizens is not *whether* considerations of justice and punishment should play a role in sentencing decisions but rather *what kind* and *how much* of a role these age-old factors should be accorded in a rational sentencing system.

If considerations of justice and punishment were ignored, then sentencing determinations would rationally be made on the basis of a simplistic Benthamite calculus. Sentencing officials would consider such factors as available space in prisons; likelihood that a given defendant, if permitted to remain free, would commit serious crimes; projected impact of the sentence on the future criminality of this defendant and others; and the balance of advantages and disadvantages to society of imprisoning the particular defendant. Sentencing officials do, of course, consider such factors, especially in our current age of relatively indeterminate sentencing.[13] But they also consider the gravity and culpability of the underlying crime. It is unjust to sentence a convicted robber to a longer term of imprisonment than that of a convicted murderer.[14] But where to strike the appropriate balance between "past-looking" considerations of proportionality and "future-looking" considerations of crime reduction is a question that has perennially troubled and will continue to trouble concerned people.[15]


## REHABILITATION

Isolation works directly to build walls between the allegedly dangerous and the endangered populations, and punishment works relatively directly to create disincentives to crime; rehabilitation seeks to alter the dynamics of the convicted criminal. It seeks to decrease his need to commit acquisitive crimes by increasing his ability to secure employment; it seeks to reduce his desire to commit certain crimes by redirecting his value system; it seeks to increase his control over antisocial needs and desires by restructuring his personality. To what extent these ambitious goals can be achieved in prison is much disputed. But the most recent—and exhaustive—survey of the literature on the treatment of criminals has reached the conclusion that, "[w]ith few and isolated exceptions, the rehabilitative efforts that have been reported so far have no appreciable effect on recidivism."[16]

The nature of the issues raised by rehabilitation depends to some degree on the *role* ascribed to it in sentencing theory and practice. If assumptions about a defendant's need for and society's ability to effectuate rehabilitation are used to *justify* a sentence of imprisonment or a decision not to release, the confining authority should have the burden of showing that these assumptions are valid, since in their absence the defendant presumably would remain free or serve less time. If, on the other hand, decisions on the appropriateness and duration of confinement are based exclusively on such factors as proportionality and dangerousness and if rehabilitation is merely employed as an adjunct to the process of confinement, it does not have to be justified in the same way. The practice of imposing rehabilitation on a prisoner without his consent or by employing threats concerning duration and/or conditions of confinement raises serious questions akin to those presented by using rehabilitation to justify confinement. But simply making rehabilitative facilities *available* to prisoners serving sentences justified on other "legitimate grounds"[17] raises less compelling issues.[18]

In the United States today, rehabilitative assumptions play some role in determining whether and for how long defendants have to be confined, but the precise weight given to such assumptions varies enormously among judges. Moreover, the rhetoric of rehabilitation is sometimes used to justify confinement decisions that are based, in actuality, on an assumed need for isolation or on a desire to punish. But a rational discussion of rehabilitation requires that distinctions be drawn among the various roles that rehabilitative assumptions may play in a sentencing structure.

## COMBINING THE PURPOSES AND MECHANISMS OF THE CRIMINAL SENTENCE: THE "INVENTION" OF THE PRISON

Prison lends itself with equal ease to the three primary approaches to crime reduction. It isolates, punishes, and provides—in theory at least—an appropriate setting for rehabilitation.

This coalescence of functions also gives rise to confusion. To dispel this confusion, one might postulate a system in which imprisonment may be used *only* to isolate, never to punish or to rehabilitate; punishment would have to take the form of either a monetary deprivation (such as a fine or a disqualification) or an immediate imposition of physical pain or dismemberment; rehabilitation could be compelled *only* on an outpatient basis and never in prison. Under this system only those convicted defendants[19] who were demonstrably dangerous could be imprisoned and only as long as they remained dangerous.[20]

The number of convicted persons imprisoned under such a system would almost certainly be lower than the number imprisoned today, although the amount of the reduction would depend on the type and degree of dangerousness required for confinement. If, for example, only convicts with a very high likelihood (say, 80 percent or more) of inflicting physical harm could be confined, then prison populations would be significantly reduced. If, on the other hand, all convicts with any significant likelihood (say, 20 percent or more) of inflicting physical, psychological, or property harm could be confined, then the reduction (if any) would be far more modest.

Such a system would force sentencing judges to think harder about the intended purpose or purposes of a criminal sentence. They could not order imprisonment if the purpose were either strictly rehabilitative or strictly punitive whether for deterrence or for retaliation. Only if the judge concluded—on the basis of satisfactory evidence—that the convicted defendant met the standard of dangerousness could he order confinement.[21]

In practice, of course, difficulties and confusion would persist. What if a sentencing judge concluded that a given defendant met the standard of dangerousness and *also* deserved serious punishment: could he then order physical and/or financial punishment *over and above* that inherent in the confinement, or could he conclude that the confinement satisfied both purposes? What if the judge concluded that a defendant who met the standard of dangerousness also needed rehabilitation: could he then compel rehabilitative efforts during the period of confinement, or would such efforts have to await the convict's release? Once the law permitted sentencing functions to be combined—as they surely would be in real life—analytic confusions would be generated. But the requirement that judges articulate and justify their sentencing decisions by reference to the specific purpose of each sentence would probably contribute some clarification.

Such a system would also reserve the resource of imprisonment—expensive for both the imprisoned individual and society at large—for those convicted defendants whose imprisonment produced the most demonstrable results.

But this system would deprive society of a major deterrent against crimes committed by "nondangerous" and "nonrecidivating" offenders—white-collar, governmental, and political criminals—who are often uniquely sensitive to the stigma and deprivation of imprisonment and to the risk of being imprisoned along with "common" criminals. It would also deprive us of the important educational and symbolic message that the crimes usually committed by the wealthy and powerful are as serious and as destructive of important values as are crimes of violence, which most often are committed by the poor.

Imprisonment only for potentially dangerous criminals would deny society the use of imprisonment as a punishment; hence, it might lead to the creation and employment of other forms of punishment that might be deemed less civilized. Whether whipping should be considered less civilized than imprisonment is a question that is receiving renewed interest in some places, but the "cruel and unusual punishment" clause of our state and federal constitutions—at least as it is currently interpreted—may impose serious constraints upon the employment of corporal punishments. On the other hand, if alternate punishments were not severe, non-dangerous criminals convicted of serious crimes would find themselves treated more leniently than dangerous criminals convicted of less serious crimes; and the seriousness of nonviolent, nonrecidivating crimes would be unduly diminished. For example, fines—especially at their current levels—are widely regarded as slaps on the wrist or criminal-license fees.

Current sentencing practices (especially as they relate to the sentence of imprisonment) are inconsistent, but the problems that result do not lend themselves to simple solutions. And imprisonment is likely to remain the dominant formal response to conviction for serious crime, not only for dangerous criminals but also for nondangerous criminals convicted of serious crimes.

## II / Three Models of Criminal Sentencing

The history of criminal sentencing in the United States has been a history of shift in institutional power and in the theories that have guided the exercise of such power. In each period, one of three sentencing models has predominated, either the legislative, judicial, or administrative model. These are so called in recognition of the institution or the group of policy makers and exercises the power to imprison and to determine the length of imprisonment. Although incarcerative powers usually are shared by several persons or agencies, it is nevertheless possible to postulate pure sentencing models.

In the *legislatively fixed model*, the legislature determines that conviction for a given crime warrants a given term of imprisonment. For example, a first offender convicted of armed robbery must be sentenced to five years' imprisonment. There is no judicial or administrative discretion under this model; the legislature has authorized but one sentence.

In practice, there is still discretion at various points in this process. The police and prosecutor generally have wide discretion to determine the charge—whether the taking was a robbery or some lesser form of larceny, for example, or whether the means of committing the crime included the requisite type of weapon. Also, the executive generally has discretion to commute or pardon. In theory, however, the legislatively fixed sentence model is the least discretionary in the sense that the sentence is determined in advance of the crime and without knowing the identity of the criminal. But since the legislature has enormous discretion to determine which crimes deserve what punishments and since it is widely known what kinds of persons generally commit what kinds of crimes, racial and other kinds of prejudice tend to play a role in determining punishments for different typical crimes. In the *judicially fixed model*, the legislature determines the general range of imprisonment for a given crime. For example, a first offender convicted of armed robbery shall be sentenced to no less than 1 and no more than 10 years' imprisonment. The sentencing judge must fix a determinate sentence within that range: "I sentence the defendant to five years' imprisonment." Once this sentence is fixed, it cannot be increased or reduced by any parole board or adult authority; the defendant must serve for five years. (This model does not consider good-time provisions or other relatively automatic reductions, nor does it consider commutation or pardon.)

Under this model, discretion is vested in the sentencing judge; how much is vested depends on the range of imprisonment authorized by the legislature. On the day he is sentenced, however, the defendant knows precisely how long he will serve; there is no discretion vested in the parole board or prison authorities.

In the *administratively fixed model*, the legislature sets an extremely wide permissible range of imprisonment for a given crime. A first-offense armed robber, for example, shall be sentenced to a term of one day to life. The sentencing judge must—or may—impose the legislatively determined sentence: "You are sentenced to one day to life." The actual duration of the sentence is decided by an administrative agency while the prisoner is serving his sentence. For example, after five years of imprisonment, the adult authority decides that the prisoner is ready for release.

Under this model, vast discretion is vested in the administrative agency and in the prison authorities. On the day he is sentenced, the defendant does not know how long he will have to serve, although he probably can make an educated guess based on past practices.

The literature on the practice and purposes of sentencing over the last two centuries is surprisingly spotty; authoritative historical accounts are lacking.[1] Nevertheless, it is possible to discern three separate historical periods characterized by the markedly different sentencing systems that have been outlined.

There has never been a time, of course, when a pure model was actually in operation. Discretionary powers have operated either overtly or covertly to determine the actual punishments meted out to offenders. A particularly significant deviation at all times and in all models has resulted from plea bargaining, under which the sentence is determined (or at least critically affected) by negotiations between the prosecutor and the defense attorney.

Plea negotiations take a different form depending on the model. For example, where the sentence is legislatively fixed, the objective of the negotiations will probably be to reduce the charge from a more serious to a less serious one (thus directly reducing the legistatively determined sentence). Where the sentence is judicially determined, the objective will probably be to reduce the sentence imposed by the judge. Where the sentence is administratively determined, the objective will probably be to have the prosecutor put a good word in with the parole board. There can be no practical understanding of any sentencing system without an appreciation of the role played by plea bargaining.

Historically, the periods during which the three models predominated have overlapped one another considerably. Indeed, as it currently operates, the administrative model could be more accurately characterized as a mixed discretionary model, since enormous discretion is still vested in the sentencing court as well as in the administrative release authority. In general, the legislature determines the general range of sentences for a particular crime (imprisonment from 3 to 10 years for first-offense armed robbery), the judge may select any sentence within that range (say, 5 years), and the parole board may then release him after a specific percentage of his sentence has been served (say, one-third).

The philosophies and legal structures that shape most of our current sentencing practices are hardly of recent origin. Today's indeterminate sentences and the administrative systems that regulate release are the result of reformative goals first articulated more than a hundred years ago at the celebrated 1870 convention of the National Prison Association at Cincinnati. The Declaration of Principles passed by that remarkable gathering are infused with a humanitarian optimism concerning the future of penology and the prison.[2] Rehabilitation of the incarcerated offender was to be the institution's most important role. Increased public financial support and increased professional diagnostic and treatment staff, it was felt, would surely result in successful cures for the great number of prisoners, who could then be released at the appropriate moment to begin the transition to constructive, responsible citizenship outside the walls of the institution. A flexible sentencing system, which vested decision-making powers in correctional personnel, was deemed essential so that prisoners could be released or detained according to informed judgments concerning their rehabilitation or likely recidivism. Much of the current attention directed to correctional change, in effect, is a call for full implementation of that Declaration of Principles.

## III / From Punishment to Rehabilitation

The concept of rehabilitation, as we now understand it, would have been entirely alien to the early colonists, whose Calvinistic view of the depraved nature of man effectively eliminated rehabilitation as a possibility. Society's duty was simply to punish the offender—swiftly, publicly, and often quite harshly.

Colonial Americans used a variety of techniques other than incarceration to protect their communities from the threat of crime. One effective method for both preventing and punishing offenses was the enforcement of settlement laws; unwanted individuals were simply "warned out" of town (excluded) by the constable. Specific crimes were punished, according to the colonial criminal codes, with relatively specific penalties. Economic crimes were usually punished by a system of fines in addition to orders of restitution.[1]

Offenders who could not pay were sentenced to forced labor, whipped, placed in the stocks, or perhaps branded with a symbol for their offense.[2] These same corporal penalties were also deemed appropriate for a wide variety of petty offenses.

Colonial criminal codes sometimes gave the magistrate a measure of discretion concerning, for example, the duration of an offender's stay in the stocks or the pillory. But, in general, punishments were legislatively prescribed with some precision. Often that prescription was death. Petty offenders who were not deterred by the whip and who again committed a crime were subject to capital punishment. How else could the colonists deter repeated offenses by prisoners who regarded the threat of corporal punishment an insufficient deterrent?[3] The death sentence was mandated for a broad range of crimes committed by first offenders. Such an inflexible system of punishments no doubt resulted in a large measure of jury nullification. Realizing that conviction necessarily meant the imposition of a disproportionately harsh penalty, juries probably returned not-guilty verdicts in a significant number of cases. On the other hand, penalties imposed on many first offenders were quite lenient, since imprisonment was not a widely available alternative. The colonists' law enforcement system thus vacillated between overly lenient and overly harsh punishments. The process lacked a flexible penalty structure that could be modified to fit the seriousness of a range of offenses.

Incarceration as a punishment for the purposes of rehabilitation was practically nonexistent. Although some communities had local jails, these did not house convicted offenders serving criminal sentences. Jails were populated by people awaiting punishment—defendants who were being held for trial or who had been unable to raise sufficient funds to pay court-imposed fines and were enduring a term of forced labor in order to earn money to pay those debts. The idea of confinement-as-punishment had been tried in only one colony, and the experiment there was short-lived. In 1682, a Pennsylvania statute provided for the creation of "workhouses for felons, thiefs, vagrants, and loose, abusive, and idle persons."[4] These institutions were to hold convicted persons, not simply those awaiting trial. However, the Pennsylvania criminal code was altered in 1718, and fines and corporal punishment replaced the still nascent concept of confinement (and enforced labor) as an appropriate form of criminal sentence.

Thus, with few exceptions, criminal sentencing in the colonial period followed a strict legislative model. Statutes dictated relatively fixed sentences—the whip, the stocks, fines, death.Although magistrates sometimes had a modicum of discretion concerning the duration of corporal punishments,[5] for the most part, the system was characterized by inflexibility.

*POST-REVOLUTION OPTIMISM:*
*INCARCERATIVE REFORM*

After the Revolution, the states began to shed the philosophy that had guided colonial views of proper and effective sentencing methods and the criminal statutes that had resulted. This was partly in response to Enlightenment rationalism and partly in revulsion against the British origins of inherited criminal codes.

The old codes seemed crude and inhumane, unbefitting a young nation that had abandoned its dark Calvinist origins and was filled with an optimism that man could be improved, that his nature was not intractably evil, and that rational government could further the public welfare through just laws. Furthermore, it was quite clear that the colonial system, even with its sharp escalation of penalties, had failed to prevent recidivism or to check a generally rising crime rate. Having left behind the theory that sin was a natural human phenomenon, some Americans came to believe that perhaps the outmoded dysfunctional codes were themselves contributing to criminal deviance. A more rational statutory delineation of the criminal laws and punishments, it was thought, should occasion a more rational—i.e., less deviant—population.

From about 1790 to 1820, several states undertook rather complete revisions of their criminal codes. These revisions reflected the views that certainty of punishment is more important than severity of punishment and that the proper amount or duration of punishment should be proportionate to the social harm occasioned by the underlying offense.[6]

These were the classical views of the role of criminal sanctions, as clearly expressed by Cesare Beccaria in his influential 1764 tract, *On Crimes and Punishments.* Beccaria argued that harsh laws not only were unbecoming to a democratic society but also were self-defeating. Beccaria's moral, quickly adopted by the new American nation, was a straightforward one:

The certainty of punishment, even if it be moderate, will always make a stronger impression than the fear of another which is more terrible but combined with the hope of impunity. . . . Do you want to prevent crimes? See to it that the laws are clear and simple and that the entire force of a nation is united in their defense.[7]

State legislatures enacted new codes that drastically limited the death penalty—the most inhumane and most often disproportionate of the inherited English criminal sanctions. Flogging, whipping, branding, and other corporal punishments also were abolished in many jurisdictions. In place of violent physical penalties, the states developed a new and quite innovative form of criminal sentence: imprisonment, often with idealistic goals for the offender's benefit.

When first proposed as a sentencing mechanism, imprisonment was seen as a reformative policy merely because it served as a substitute for capital punishment. However, incarceration rather quickly developed its own justifications as an intrinsically reformative institution. Through carefully calibrated systems of discipline, labor, and religious exhortation, the penitentiary could "cure" the offender of his criminogenic pathology. Because man was now seen as a rational, willful actor, surely rational laws plus rational punishment systems would cure a condition (crime) that was conceived of as a disease of the moral faculty.

The underpinnings of this optimistic view of incarcerative reform were first set forth in 1787 at a meeting at the Philadelphia home of Benjamin Franklin. An influential group gathered there to hear Dr. Benjamin Rush deliver a paper concerning the establishment of a modern prison system. Rush urged a prison program that would (1) establish various inmate classification programs, for purposes of both inmate housing assignments and various treatment plans; (2) devise a self-supporting institutional system based on inmate piecework and agriculture; and (3) impose indeterminate periods of confinement on inmates who would then be released on the basis of evidence of their progress toward rehabilitation.[8] The Philadelphia Society for Alleviating the

Miseries of Public Prisons was organized to implement Dr. Rush's idealistic program. In 1790, the Society succeeded in prevailing upon the state legislature to authorize the remodeling of Philadelphia's Walnut Street Jail in order to fashion a prison into a "cellhouse" that could serve as a proving ground for the new theory of individualized reformative incarceration.

## DOMINANCE AND DIFFICULTIES OF THE JUDICIAL MODEL

Over the next few decades, as state codes were reworked, capital and corporal punishments gave way to sentences of imprisonment. But the theory of criminal sentencing underwent very little substantive revision. Numerous large penitentiaries were constructed and quickly populated, both with those who would previously have been executed and with those who would previously have been punished by the stocks and whip. Legislatures gave courts discretion to impose sentences that could then be altered only by the executive's pardoning power, though these ranges were rather narrow compared to today's legislatively authorized punishments. Some nineteenth-century statutes set out different gradations of offenses that had formerly had only one broad definition and fixed punishment.

Throughout almost the entire century, the judicial mode for criminal sentencing was predominant. The difficulty was that this prevailing model was in serious conflict with the developing rhetoric of reformative incarceration.

The legislature set the outside limits within which sentencing discretion could be exercised, but the statutes did not set out specific, detailed criteria to guide judicial sentencing. The sentence imposed by the court upon the individual offender was fixed: it did not include a minimum term or a maximum term subject to later decisions by other institutions or persons such as wardens. A sentence of two years meant precisely 730 days—unless, of course, a pardon or some sort of commutation was forthcoming from the executive branch.[9]

Despite hortatory calls to vocational and spiritual betterment, an inmate's response in the prison environment mattered not at all when it came to the duration of his sentence: Whether or not he was a model prisoner, he was probably going to serve the precise sentence pronounced by the court. He could not earn an early release from his keeper, and he could not be punished with detention beyond the date already set by the court for his release.

The length of judicially imposed sentences was almost invariably a function of how the court (and, in the first instance, the legislature) viewed the seriousness of the crime committed. Courts, as sentencing institutions, rarely concerned themselves with correctional goals other than simple punishment for a particular criminal act. If the conviction was for the felony of assault, a New York court, on "a consideration of all the circumstances" of the case, could sentence an offender to imprisonment in solitary confinement at hard labor or to "simple" incarceration for any term up to 14 years.[10] The relevant circumstances for the court would probably have included such considerations as the ferocity of the attack and the defendant's motive (and perhaps the likelihood that the defendant would commit assault again). It would have been highly unlikely for the court to fix a sentence on the basis of a factor such as the offender's predicted good behavior in the institution.

As the judicial model functioned during the nineteenth century, courts were exercising sentencing discretion largely on the basis of judgments concerning particular offenses. The courts were seemingly unconcerned with the institutional setting in which the offender would serve out the judicially fixed term. Apparently, there was little communication between the judiciary and prison administrators concerning the purposes and philosophy of incarceration. Courts saw themselves as punishers: the role was unambiguous, uncomplicated, and straightforward.

Wardens, on the other hand, had more difficulty articulating precisely what goals their institutions were pursuing and what methods were most appropriate. Expressing belief that their wards could be cured, the managers of these new fortresses engaged in a fervent, protracted, and (to the modern mind) quite bizarre debate concerning the relative efficacy of convicts silently laboring in groups or in individual cells. Which was better? The Auburn System, in which inmates were released from their separate cells during the day for hard labor in groups? Or the Pennsylvania System, in which inmates were at all times confined in individual cells where they worked and presumably repented in total solitude? The seriousness of the debate was all the more remarkable inasmuch as the two systems were so clearly more similar than dissimilar.

There seemed to be little concern at all with examining what was, to the prisoners, the basic fact concerning their incarceration, namely, its time limit as set by the court. On the day they were deposited at the institution, prisoners knew how long they had to remain. The keepers could not shorten or lengthen the term. Such a system hardly offered any strong incentives for an inmate to participate willingly in the strict programs of deprivation that were touted as the correct paths to righteousness.

*ATTENTION TURNS TO SENTENCING REFORM*

By mid-century, the Auburn-Pennsylvania controversy no longer held the attention of persons involved in correctional planning. The penitentiaries' experimentation with various types of discipline, deprivation, training, and labor clearly had failed. Inmates were not being reformed. In fact, the prison population was increasingly made up of the most hardened and practiced criminals, those least subject to rehabilitative efforts or programs.[11] The courts' sentencing power was being exercised so that the punishment of prison incarceration was imposed upon only the most serious offenders; younger, perhaps more malleable defendants received shorter sentences in local jails or never suffered any deprivation of liberty at all. The penitentiaries were obviously failing at their proclaimed purpose. Maintaining institutional order was becoming more and more difficult. Problems of custody and control preempted concerns about what precise mixture of Bible reading and isolation would lead to repentant vows to begin a new life. This confrontation with failure brought about a dramatic lowering of expectations. The prison reformers did not openly abandon the goal of reforming the offender but turned their attention from questions of incarcerative techniques to issues of sentencing structure. The reformers perceived that the prison's failure had resulted from an inappropriate vesting of power in the court. How could a judge, on the basis of only brief observation of the defendant and only scanty knowledge of his character, know what period of imprisonment would be necessary in order to ensure that the offender was released only when he was prepared to lead a law-abiding life? Would not such judgments be more appropriately made by prison officials or other experts in penology, who could act on the basis of fuller information and a broader understanding of the nature and causes of criminal behavior? In their sentences, courts punished crime. But the penologists of this era believed that prisons, in executing those sentences, should focus on the needs of the individual criminal. They viewed the judicially fixed sentence as quite dysfunctional and a major obstacle both to rational rehabilitative plans and to efforts to protect society by keeping likely recidivists incarcerated until they ceased to be dangerous.

The reformers' argument criticized judicial sentencing power for focusing excessively on the defendant's guilt or innocence regarding a particular crime instead of paying attention to such matters as the offender's possible danger to the community. S. J. May, a leading prison reformer, made the following argument in the 1847 report of the Prison Association of New York:

> You ask me for how long a time he should be sentenced to such confinement? Obviously, it seems to me, until the evil disposition is removed from his heart; until his disqualification to go at large no longer exists; that is, until he is a reformed man. How long this may be, no human sagacity certainly can predetermine. I have therefore for many years been of the opinion that no discretion should be conferred on our judges in regard to the length of a convict's confinement; that no term of time should be

affixed to any sentence of the court. The offender should be adjudged to undergo the duress and the discipline of the prison-house, not for weeks, months, or years, but until that end for which alone he should be put there is accomplished; that is, until reformation has evidently been affected.

All attempts by our legislators and ministers of criminal jurisprudence to decide upon the degree of criminality in different offenders must be abortive, because only Omniscience is competent to do this. Even if human wisdom can ascertain the different qualities of evil flowing through society from the commission of different crimes, surely no legislators or judges can be wise enough to determine the comparative wickedness of those who have committed these crimes. The man who has been convicted only of a petty larceny may be found, when subjected to prison discipline, a much more incorrigible offender than another who committed highway robbery, burglary, or arson. One of the greatest improvements in the administration of our penal code would be to withhold from the judges all discretion as to the time for which convicts shall be confined.[12]

In other words, courts should logically be divested of their sentencing powers; instead, various scientific experts should make all judgments concerning the length of a criminal's incarceration. This is the argument, of course, for the establishment of the third sentencing model, the administrative model, in which legislatively permissible sentences are extremely broad, judicial sentences are indeterminate, and release dates are set by an executive board at some point after the defendant begins his term of incarceration.

The indeterminate sentence was the logical solution to the tension between judicially fixed sentences and institutional goals of motivating inmates to become law-abiding citizens and to behave well in prison, with release occurring when they achieve a cure. Even during the period of the judicial model, reform of the individual offender had been posited by prison administrators as the goal of their institutions. Such a goal was most comfortably expressed within a system that actually referred directly to that goal in determining the length of sentence.

# IV/Indeterminate Sentencing and the Administrative Model

The 1870 National Prison Congress gave dramatic expression to the "enlightened" view of a sentencing system that would strongly reinforce rehabilitative rather than punitive purposes. The Declaration of Principles called for a variety of penal reforms, among them a radical alteration of the existing sentencing structure. It paid lip service to the punitive rationale for sentencing in stating that "crime is an intentional violation of duties imposed by law" and "[p]unishment is suffering . . . in expiation of the wrong done." But more importantly, it also described crime as "a moral disease, of which punishment is the remedy." And it went on to say:

> The efficiency of the remedy is a question of social therapeutics, a question of the fitness and the measure of the dose. . . . [P]unishment is directed not to the crime but the criminal. . . . The supreme aim of prison discipline is the reformation of criminals, not the infliction of vindictive suffering.[1]

With "reformation" as the uncompromised goal of the prison, it followed that release should be effected only upon its achievement. Thus, the Congress declared that

> peremptory sentences ought to be replaced by those of indeterminate duration—sentences limited only by satisfactory proof of reformation should be substituted for those measured by mere lapse of time.[2]

This principle was most strongly urged by Zebulon Brockway, then the superintendent of the Elmira Reformatory in New York, who addressed the delegates on "The Ideal of a True Prison System." His ideal was premised on the indeterminate sentence. The "indeterminate sentence" and the "indeterminate reformatory" were the methods by which the reformation of the criminal and the protection of society could be most effectively achieved. Brockway rejected vengeance (pure punishment) as unjust and deterrence as a failure and in its place proposed a system of confinement under which

> all persons in a state, who are convicted of crimes or offenses before a competent court, shall be deemed wards of the state and shall be committed to the custody of the board of guardians, until, in their judgment, they may be returned to society with ordinary safety and in accord with their own highest welfare.[3]

Scorning "sickly sentimentalism" and "popular philanthrop[y]," Brockway characterized his proposal as hard realism, designed to "guarantee" the "safety" of society "from further depredations" of convicted criminals.[4] Nevertheless, his proposal for indefinite sentencing was entirely congruent with the benign rhetoric of the enthusiasts of rehabilitation.

Brockway's approach was stated in the extreme in an influential article by Charlton T. Lewis in the *Yale Law Journal*[5] at the turn of the century. Lewis reflected the evolving view of the indeterminate sentence in the United States when he stated that it was the only "right method of dealing with crime" and that its governing principle should be that "no man be imprisoned unless it is clear that his freedom is dangerous to others, and that when once imprisoned, no man be freed until the danger has ceased."[6] Considerations of deterrence, retribution, and justice were ignored; rehabilitation, which he called reconciliation, was only one means of reducing the criminal's dangerousness. He advocated that the crime itself have "no bearing upon the questions"[7] since confinement is not "punishment for this offense."[8]

The first explicit indeterminate-sentence law for crimes in the United States had been enacted at the behest of Zebulon Brockway in Michigan in 1869. It was extremely limited, applying only to "common prostitutes" and providing for a three-year sentence that could be terminated at any time at the discretion of the inspectors of the Detroit House of Correction.[9] (The maximum punishment for prostitution at that time was far less than three years.) Eight years later, Brockway secured the enactment of the first indeterminate-sentence law of more widespread penal application. His original proposal was for an indeterminate-sentence law "without limitation," but "neither public sentiment in general nor the views of the legislators would accept this."[10]

It was New York in the following year that adopted a modified provision typical of the statutes later enacted in most states. The New York law limited the term of the sentence to "the maximum term provided by law for the crime for which the prisoner was convicted and sentenced," but left the determination of the exact amount of time to be served to the managers of the reformatory. Here is the way in which this authority was granted by the statute:

> Every sentence to the reformatory of a person hereafter convicted of a felony or other crime shall be a general sentence to imprisonment in the New York State reformatory at Elmira and the courts of this state imposing such sentence shall not fix or limit the duration thereof. The term of such imprisonment of any person so convicted and sentenced shall be terminated by the managers of the reformatory, as authorized by this act; but such imprisonment shall not exceed the maximum term provided by law for the crime for which the prisoner was convicted and sentenced.[11]

The various forms of indeterminate sentence are practically unlimited. For example, Edward Lindsey identified and described 13 variations in existence in 1922. By that time, only four states were without some form of indeterminate sentencing or parole system, both of which were functionally similar to the indeterminate sentence.[12]

## THE ADMINISTRATIVE MODEL TAKES OVER

Ironically, by the time that indeterminate-sentencing structures had been established in many jurisdictions, the belief in man's ability to better his moral faculties was giving way to new forms of physiological and ethnic determinism. The new criminologists suggested that some, if not most, criminal "types" could not overcome their propensities for deviant behavior. Accordingly, the indeterminate sentence and parole systems could be used to prolong the incarceration of those offenders felt to be incurable.

According to this view, prison and parole authorities, together with the various diagnostic and treatment specialists and their staffs, were unquestionably in the best position to evaluate an inmate. Judging "the potential menace of [his] pathological personality to the community at large" was surely no job for the judiciary, said H. E. Barnes.

It is necessary for us to come to realize the fact that every dictate of medical and social science unquestionably indicates that lawyers and courts have no more proper function in dealing with criminals (using this term in a scientific sense) than they have in taking full charge of the treatment of mentally defective and insane types. . . . As soon as science—natural, biological, medical, psychological and social—comes to be applied to our methods of handling the delinquent classes, it will be seen that the function of the criminal law ends with the mere formal legal or judicial supervision of the forms of procedure, comparable to the judicial supervision at present of the processes of committing an alleged insane person to a hospital for the insane and approving his discharge after a cure has been effected.[13]

In 1915, in an editorial entitled "The Parole System: A Means of Protection," the *Journal of the American Institute of Criminal Law and Criminology* advanced various arguments for continued support of the system of parole and indeterminate sentencing. "The parole system," it said, "had been accompanied by an increased average time served in prison." Nor was there any evidence "that society is endangered thus far through unwarranted parole of habitual criminals; rather the reverse, but their closer detention can do no harm."[14] Medical terminology and methodology began to infuse the functioning of the prison system. Ideally, inmates were carefully "classified" (diagnosed), and treatment plans were prescribed for individual conditions; prisoners' responses to rehabilitative programs were constantly monitored and evaluated; upon recovery from their criminal disease, they were paroled. Of course, some criminal syndromes had no known cures. Such inmates, unable to demonstrate that the symptoms and cause of their disorders had somehow disappeared, had to remain in prison to serve out their full sentences. The indeterminate sentence was essential to the workings of this system. The large amount of discretionary power vested in correctional and parole personnel was necessary in order to give the clinicians (psychiatrists and psychologists, educators, social workers, and employment counselors) the needed leeway to tailor their efforts to each individual prisoner.

This system is essentially still with us. Indeed, the administrative sentencing model with its indeterminate sentence is the dominant mechanism of involuntary confinement currently employed in the United States. A considerable percentage of incarcerated prisoners are, of course, awaiting trial; but pretrial confinement is not considered here, even though admittedly it raises some problems relevant to indeterminate sentencing. During 1973, the most recent year for which statistics are available, 75 percent of the 105,000 convicted felons released from prison left via "conditional release"—in most cases, on parole.[15] In all likelihood, the proportion of inmates being granted conditional releases (as opposed to unconditional discharges) is somewhat higher today.[16] It is extremely rare for a convicted criminal or a committed patient to know, at the time judgment is formally imposed by the court, precisely how long he actually will be retained in confinement.

Until very recently, criticisms of the correctional sentencing system were largely to the effect that insufficient resources have been directed to our prisons. If only there were more and better trained counselors, more relevant job-training equipment, more parole personnel to conduct more thorough release hearings, etc., then surely the system would finally work. But now more searching and far-reaching criticism is being directed at the concept itself; the model is no longer unquestioningly accepted.

## THE EMERGING ATTACK ON INDETERMINATE SENTENCING

Skepticism toward the rehabilitation-therapy model of confinement, of which indeterminate sentencing is a part, had begun to develop by the mid-1960s.[17] The indeterminate sentence has always been justified by analogy to other forms of indeterminate confinement, such as commitment of the mentally ill. Cesare Lombroso directly analogized indeterminate imprisonment of the "born criminal" to confinement of the insane.[18] This was echoed recently in the statement by a supporter of indeterminate confinement that no one "questions the power of the state to commit to institutions mentally unbalanced persons who become dangerous to the peace and safety of the community."[19] But it was this very power of the government to confine allegedly dangerous persons for preventive and therapeutic reasons that scholars and civil libertarians were beginning to question. Much of this skepticism was generated by the complaints of those serving indeterminate sentences.[20] These complaints began to be reflected in the literature and stimulated criticisms of indeterminate sentencing by academics and law reformers.[21] The growing skepticism among courts, legislators, and scholars during the last decade is in part a product of recent studies demonstrating that dangerousness is difficult to predict[22] and that the effectiveness of treatment in reducing recidivism is open to serious question.[23]

In 1971, the first of three particularly influential books

criticizing the indeterminate sentence appeared. This was a report prepared for the American Friends Service Committee under the guidance of Professor Caleb Foote of Berkeley, recommending the abolition of indeterminate sentencing and the adoption of a system that makes punishment proportional to the act committed.[24] (It advocated, however, the retention of good-time reductions of sentence with proper safeguards.) The Friends' report focuses squarely on the preventive aspects of indeterminate sentencing in noting that the "concept of preventive detention has for a century been a raison d'etre for a system of indeterminate sentencing."[25] Indeed, it goes even beyond this in asserting that in the United States today most persons who are sentenced to imprisonment are so sentenced *primarily* for preventive reasons:

> Any prisoner denied leniency by a judge or parole board is likely to be imprisoned under a policy of preventive detention. Many, of course, are detained for retributive or general deterrence purposes. But for what is probably the majority, confinement is the result of a decision that the prisoner is not yet safe enough to release.[26]

Any form of preventive detention, the report concluded, is "a major setback in the struggle for justice" because it means imprisoning "many persons who would not have committed a crime if released, along with the few who would have."[27]

Jessica Mitford's more popular work, *Kind and Usual Punishment*, focuses particularly on indeterminate sentencing as it is practiced in California. After describing its humane-sounding qualities, she poses the following questions:

> Why, then is [the indeterminate sentence] denounced by the supposed beneficiaries—prisoners and parolees— from coast to coast, its abolition one of the focal demands of the current prison rebellion? And why is it coming under increasing attacks from those criminologists, sociologists, lawyers, legislators who have taken the trouble to look closely at the prison scene and have informed themselves at first hand about the day-to-day realities of prison life?[28]

Among the abuses causing this outcry, says Mitford, are "much longer sentences for most prisoners than would normally be imposed by judges"[29] and "total arbitrariness of the bureaucracy that rules every aspect of their existence,"[30] notably the duration of their confinement. The most scholarly and thoughtful of these recent works is Judge Marvin Frankel's *Criminal Sentences—Law without Order*, which is a general critique of sentencing, especially in the federal courts. Finding that "the movement toward indeterminacy in sentencing is broad and powerful,"[31] Frankel articulates a "minority position." "Indeterminate sentencing, as thus far employed and justified," he says, "has produced more cruelty and injustice than the benefits its supporters envisage."[32] Frankel doubts that rehabilitation—an important justification of indeterminacy—is possible in most cases. He opts for a "presumption . . . in favor of a definite sentence, known and justified on the day of sentencing [and probably much shorter than our sentences tend to run]." There should be

> a burden of justifying an indeterminate sentence in any particular case—a burden to be satisfied by concrete reasons and a concrete program for the defendant involved. The justification . . . would consist of identified needs and resources for effective rehabilitation.[33]

Frankel is also critical of other justifications for indeterminate sentencing, including the continued confinement of the dangerous offender. He raises questions "about the possibility of identifying with reasonable accuracy the dangerous individual."[34] Moreover, even if "we knew . . . how to detect who is dangerous," the question of what level of risk a society should be willing to tolerate—and who should make this critical judgment—would still remain. Though Frankel reluctantly accepts the need for some indeterminacy "in the service of incapacitating dangerous people," here, too, he would invoke a heavy presumption in favor of a fixed sentence in any given case.

# V/Disparate Results from Indeterminate Sentencing

Today's mixed discretionary sentencing model, based on the indeterminate sentence, places most discretionary powers in the hands of both judicial and parole authorities, with predictable consequences. Determinacy and indeterminacy in sentencing are, of course, matters of degree. A sentence is more or less indeterminate to the extent that the amount of time actually to be served is decided not by the judge at the time the sentence is imposed but rather by an administrative board while the sentence is being served. A judicially imposed sentence of life imprisonment with no possibility of parole (or other discretionary reduction) is entirely determinate. A sentence of one day to life—the actual duration to be determined by the parole board after service of sentence has commenced—is entirely indeterminate.

In between lies a wide range of sentences. A sentence of not less than 5 or more than 10 years is partially indeterminate; although its maximum and minimum are fixed at the time of sentencing, the actual time to be served within those limits will be decided subsequently by some administrative authority. Another form of indeterminate sentence is the term of imprisonment for what appears to be a fixed period, say 10 years, but is subject to the normal rules of parole; this makes it advisable for an administrative board to authorize release after a statutorily prescribed percentage of the sentence has been served. Thus, all sentences subject to parole (the vast majority of prison sentences imposed in the United States today) are indeterminate to some degree. (See Appendix for a more extended analysis of the important differences that tend to occur according to the nature of the sentencing decisions.)

As with all complex human institutions, a certain predictability eventually sets in, and a special language develops. In practical terms, most criminal sentences fall closer to the determinate than the indeterminate pole of the continuum. Therefore, most prisoners, with the help of their lawyers, can make a fairly accurate calculation of the amount of time that they will serve if they behave well in prison.[1]

A convicted federal first offender sentenced to 3 years for extortion, for example, can generally expect to serve approximately 19 months in prison.[2] Predictability will depend on a number of factors, including the range of the available sentence, the seriousness (particularly the violence) of the underlying offense, the prior record of the offender, the publicity attached to the particular crime or criminal, and the policies of the releasing agency.

Despite this modicum of predictability, the overall result of this essentially discordant situation has been a glaring disparity in sentencing. This is a staggering reality no matter how "disparity" is defined, whether in terms of unequal sentences for similar crimes, similar defendants, or similar defendants convicted of similar crimes. There are no comprehensive national sentencing statistics to present a full picture, but all the data that do exist demonstrate that unjustifiable disparity is a prominent result of discretionary decision making.

## STATISTICAL EVIDENCE

In 1971, the Federal Bureau of Prisons compiled state-by-state statistics of the sentences imposed by state and local courts on "first releases" (prisoners released for the first time on their current sentences) and the sentences actually served by these offenders.[3] As the National Commission points out, such comparisons can be "highly misleading" because a myriad of factors determines the sentence imposed and the sentence served.[4] Nevertheless, the disparities are enormous and seemingly inexplicable. Why had 62.5 percent of the Minnesota prisoners released that year served more than 10 years, while none of the Vermont inmates released had served more than 5 years? Why had 3.06 percent of the Washington prisoners released that year originally received sentences of between 1 and 5 years, while 86.1 percent of South Dakota releasees had received a sentence within that range? These comparisons are only two examples of sentencing disparity. Whatever explanation can be given, the single fact is that such vast sentencing variations cannot be justified in any rational way.

In a recent study commissioned by the judges of the U.S. Court of Appeals for the Second Circuit, 50 federal judges were given 20 identical files, drawn from actual cases, and asked what sentence they would impose on each defendant.[5] The results showed "glaring disparity." In a case involving a middle-aged union official convicted on several counts of extortionate credit transactions, one judge imposed a sentence of 20 years' imprisonment plus a $65,000 fine, whereas another judge imposed a 3-year sentence with no fine. In a case of possession of barbiturates with intent to distribute, one judge gave the defendant five years in prison, while another put him on probation. A 22-year-old alien who had illegally entered the United States received three years of imprisonment from one judge and a suspended sentence from another. One judge sentenced a defendant convicted of securities fraud to two years' imprisonment, while another fined him $2,500.

Nor can this disparity be explained by the fact that the judges in this experiment did not have flesh and blood defendants in front of them. The likelihood is that, because each judge had before him identical information about the same defendant, the disparities that exist in real life were reduced. Indeed, one of the judges included in the study recently sent shock waves through the legal community with a sentence imposed in an actual trial of a second offender convicted of stock fraud. The sentence was 10 years' imprisonment, despite a plea of guilty and cooperation with the government. This is five times the amount any judge gave a hypothetical stock defrauder in the study.[6] Numerous other studies based on actual sentencing of live defendants have found even more shocking disparities. A recent study of sentences imposed during a two-year period in Montgomery County, Ohio, disclosed that certain judges imprison defendants twice as often as other judges for the same offense. In cases of robbery, for example, one judge imposed prison sentences in 77 percent of his cases, whereas another judge imprisoned in only 17 percent of his cases.[7]

The results of a similar survey of sentences imposed in South Carolina during 1971 revealed such a wide variety of disparity that the authors found it impossible to generalize about the types of, or reasons for, unequal sentences.[8] In two marijuana cases, the same judge sentenced a white youth to one year's probation and a $400 fine; a black male received a two-year sentence; both were first offenders. A female who pled guilty to voluntary manslaughter was sentenced to 2 years' incarceration and 4 years' probation by one judge; another judge sentenced a male defendant to 21 years; again, both were first offenders. A plea of guilty to assault and battery with intent to kill brought a seven-day sentence of imprisonment and five years' probation, while a grand-larceny defendant who had stolen two suits received seven years. As the investigators aptly noted:

> More of these disparities could be catalogued but the point is made. There is no policy covering criteria or rationale or objectives for sentencing that is operative among South Carolina's circuit court judges. There are sentencing disparities in the sentencing practices of individual judges and disparities between offenses.[9]

Further, the report found disparities between the treatment of men and women, blacks and whites.

## THE FACTOR OF RACE

Perhaps race has received the closest attention as the root cause of unacceptable disparity in sentencing. In addition to revealing significant variations within and among districts, a study of federal sentences from 1967 to 1970 demonstrated that black defendants received heavier sentences than whites convicted of the same crimes. Examples: in interstate theft cases, 28 percent of white defendants and 48 percent of black defendants received prison sentences; for postal theft, the rate was 39 percent for whites and 48 percent for blacks.[10] Although subject to some methodical criticism,[11] other studies of the racial factor[12] in sentencing have almost always concluded that being black serves to enhance the punishment imposed.[13]

Studies attempting to sort out the variables accounting for disparity of sentencing patterns within a particular district or system have reached varying conclusions. One careful analysis of federal sentences imposed after trial from 1967 to 1968[14] concluded that the crime for which the defendant was convicted accounted for the greatest difference and the seriousness of the defendant's prior record had a strong impact on the sentence.[15] However, it also found that factors such as a bench trial as opposed to a jury trial and retained counsel as opposed to appointed counsel also were related to the sentencing decision.[16] Race per se seemed to play no significant role, nor did age. When sentences for a single crime—armed robbery—were examined, the results were somewhat different. Age became more important—the younger got shorter sentences. Race seemed relevant for defendants with no prior record but not for other defendants. Defendants with private counsel consistently received sentences lower than those imposed upon defendants with appointed lawyers.[17]

A sentencing study undertaken by the Office of the U.S. Attorney for the Southern District of New York in 1972[18] discerned no racial factors. Moreover, it did not take special note that, although only 36 percent of convicted white-collar criminals received a prison sentence, 53 percent of defendants convicted of nonviolent crimes were sentenced to a term of incarceration.[19]

## VI / Recent Judicial Limitations on Indeterminate Sentencing

Judicial doubts about the substantive wisdom of particular law enforcement techniques often are reflected initially by the imposition of procedural barriers. United States courts feel more comfortable placing procedural, rather than substantive, limitations on legislatively authorized programs. As Justice Harlan once said, while courts "must give the widest deference to legislative judgments" concerning the substantive criteria for confinement, the judiciary has "been understood to possess particular competence" in assessing the "necessity and wisdom of procedural guarantees."[1]

It is not surprising, therefore, that judicial limitations on indeterminate sentencing initially took the form of procedural safeguards. Three such decisions, each dealing with a different point in the indeterminate-sentence process, are dealt with in this chapter.[2] However, at least one recent decision in a state court may mark the beginning of significant substantive constraint as well on the extent of indeterminacy in sentencing. This case and other similar cases are described later in the chapter.

### JUDICIAL LIMITATIONS

In 1967, the U.S. Supreme Court imposed the first significant judicial limitation on indeterminate sentencing in *Specht v. Patterson*,[3] which involved a Colorado sex-offender act authorizing an indeterminate term of from one day to life.[4] Although Specht was convicted of indecent liberties, a crime carrying a maximum sentence of 10 years' imprisonment, he was sentenced under the sex-offender act; under Colorado law, this act can be invoked if the sentencing judge "is of the opinion that any . . . person [convicted of specified sex offenses], if at large, constitutes a threat of bodily harm to members of the public, or is an habitual offender and mentally ill."[5] The Colorado statute provided for no hearing on whether the defendant constituted a threat, and none was given Specht.

Concluding that the confinement under the sex-offender act "is criminal punishment even though it is designed not so much as retribution as it is to keep individuals from inflicting future harm,"[6] the Supreme Court held that due process requires an adversary hearing, with appropriate safeguards, before a defendant can be sentenced under the sex-offender statute. The Court's ruling did not extend, however, to all indeterminate sentencing. It went out of its way to distinguish the Colorado statute from the general run of indeterminate-sentencing provisions. The Court noted that, unlike the usual sentencing proceeding where sentence is imposed "at the end of the trial and in the same proceeding,"[7] sentencing under the sex-offender provision was a separate proceeding under another act, requiring "a new finding of fact" and "the making of a new charge leading to criminal punishment."[8]

The Court's opinion does not explain the theoretical or practical significance of this distinction. Surely Specht would have been no better off if the indeterminate-sentence provision had been part of the original criminal prosecution, as California and other state laws now provide. But unless the Court extends the reasoning of *Specht* to indeterminate sentences in general, the effect of the case will be quite limited.

*Specht* dealt with the point at which the indeterminate sentence is judicially imposed. The next important case, *Monks v. New Jersey State Parole Board*,[9] involved the point at which the actual duration of confinement is determined—the decision of the parole board to release or retain.

Monks, who was serving an indeterminate sentence for a murder he committed while a juvenile,[10] was denied parole on a number of occasions without any statement of the reasons. He then wrote the parole board asking "what was necessary to convince the board that he was a 'good parole risk'" so that he could "be in a position to behave in any way the Board expected."[11] The board replied that "as a matter of policy" it did not give reasons for its decisions.[12]

The New Jersey Supreme Court held the no-reason policy invalid and ordered the parole board to substitute "a carefully prepared rule designed generally towards affording statements of reasons on parole denials, while providing for such reasonable exceptions as may be essential to rehabilitations and the sound administration of the parole system."[13] Whether this rule will have any real impact on parole decisions, appellate review, or prisoners' attitudes remains to be seen.

At issue in the third decision were the demands of due process at the point after conditional release, when the authorities seek to reincarcerate the parolee for alleged parole violations.

As previously stated, the original proponents of the indeterminate sentence insisted that the parolee be returned to prison "on at least well-founded complaint."[14] Parole boards might, of course, hesitate to release prisoners on parole if added procedural safeguards make quick revocation difficult. However, in 1972, the U. S. Supreme Court held in *Morrissey v. Brewer*[15] that certain "basic requirements"[16] of due process must apply in revocation proceedings.[17] Noting that "studies have suggested that fair treatment of parole revocation will not result in fewer grants of parole,"[18] the Court set out the "minimum requirements" that each state must accord the parolee:

> They include (a) written notice of the claimed violations of parole; (b) disclosure to the parolee of evidence against him; (c) opportunity to be heard in person and to present witnesses and documentary evidence; (d) the right to confront and cross-examine adverse witnesses (unless the hearing officer specifically finds good cause for not allowing confrontation); (e) a "neutral and detached" hearing body such as a traditional parole board,

members of which need not be judicial officers or lawyers; and (f) a written statement by the factfinders as to the evidence relied on and reasons for revoking parole.[19]

Once again, it remains to be seen what effect this decision may have on the various stages of the indeterminate-sentencing process.

## SUBSTANTIVE LIMITATIONS

The procedural cases, while reflecting a growing concern about the abuses of indeterminate sentencing, do not impose any direct constraints on such sentences. The recent decision by the California Supreme Court *In re Lynch*[20] may mark the beginning of significant substantive constraints on the extent of indeterminacy in sentencing.

The factual setting in *Lynch* was extremely sympathetic. In 1967, Lynch, a person of "superior intellect," apparently was seen masturbating in his own car at 2:45 A.M. in the lot of a drive-in restaurant. By itself, this offense would have been a misdemeanor punishable by six months' imprisonment under California law. But because Lynch had a 1958 conviction for indecent exposure (for which he had been placed on probation), he was given an indeterminate sentence. At the time of his appeal, he had already served more than five years in prison, "three and a half of those years in the maximum security confines of Folsom."[21]

In a thoughtful and detailed opinion, the court held that an indeterminate sentence of up to life for a second indecent exposure conviction violated the "cruel or unusual punishment" prohibition of the California constitution because the maximum possible punishment was disproportionate to the underlying offense. The court was careful, however, not to strike down the indeterminate-sentence law on its face.[22] "The fault does not lie in the theory of the indeterminate sentence law," it said, "but in the unreasonably high maximum term prescribed for this offense."[23] Nevertheless, the opinion had significant implications for the entire state sentencing structure and served as a first step in bringing into sharper focus the whole issue of proportionality within the context of indeterminate sentencing and parole practices. The conventional wisdom has long been that the cruel and unusual punishment prohibition of the United States Constitution, which is analogous to the California provision, is directed primarily, if not exclusively, at the method of the punishment employed and not at its duration; it was "traditionally thought to prohibit physically torturous methods of punishment such as the rack and the screw."[24] But the California Supreme Court marshaled all the case law, state and federal, in support of the proposition that a conventional method of punishment, such as imprisonment, could be cruel or unusual if its duration were excessive in relation to the offense charged.[25] After reviewing several tests of proportionality, the court concluded that in "California a punishment may violate article I, section 6, of the Constitution if, although not cruel or unusual in its method, it is so disproportionate to the crime for which it is inflicted that it shocks the conscience and offends fundamental notions of human dignity."[26]

The court catalogued several factors to be considered in administering this open-end rule:

First, judges should examine "the nature of the offense and/or the offender, with particular regard to the degree of danger both present to society."[27] Was the crime violent or nonviolent? Were there aggravating circumstances? Was anyone injured?

Second, there should be a comparison of "the challenged penalty with the punishments prescribed in the same jurisdiction for different offenses which, by the same test, must be deemed more serious."[28] In order to employ this approach, a court would have to establish (implicitly or explicitly) a rough ranking of seriousness, place the crime in question in that order, and then determine whether other crimes that are higher on the scale of seriousness are punished less severely. For example, it would be improper to punish indecent exposure more severely than crimes such as robbery, rape, and violent assault.

Three, the challenged penalty should be compared "with the punishments prescribed for the same offense in other jurisdictions having an identical or similar constitutional provision."[29] This sort of cross-jurisdictional comparison is traditional in constitutional adjudication and is suggested by the text of the constitutional provision itself that prohibits unusual punishments.

Finding that the petitioner Lynch had met all three tests for demonstrating cruel and unusual punishment in his case, the court concluded that the disproportion between the crime of second-offense indecent exposure and the punishment of possible life imprisonment was so large as to warrant striking down the authorized penalty on its face. Such a severe penalty, said the court, even if it were only potential and even if the release authority routinely released such offenders quite early during their terms, was unconstitutionally disproportionate to the specific crime of indecent exposure. Thus, it was void.

Two years later, the California Supreme Court was called upon to apply the *Lynch* criteria to test the constitutionality of a state statute[30] applying to recidivist drug offenders. Certain of these recidivists were ineligible for parole until they had served mandatory prison sentences (10 years for a second offender and 15 years for a third offender).[31] The court took note of variations in the degree of culpability among various offenders; it was possible, the court said, to make "rational gradations of culpability . . . on the basis of the injury to the victim or to society in general."[32] The delayed parole provisions of the statute, the court held, had been imposed "without regard to the existence of such possible mitigating circumstances as the addict status of the offender, the quantity of narcotics involved, the nature of the purchaser or the purposes of the sale."[33] The court found this to be constitutionally invalid under the *Lynch* analysis, and the statute was struck down.

Two subsequent decisions by the California Supreme Court[34] dealt with actions by the California Adult Authority, the state's parole agency. They did not go so far as *Lynch* and *Foss* in invalidating entire penalty provisions because such penalties could not be constitutionally applied to the crimes they purported to punish. Nevertheless, these later cases employed the *Lynch* analysis to impose a duty upon the agency to "fix terms" for all prisoners proportional to the particular offenses committed.

In *Wingo*, the defendant had received a six-months-to-life state prison sentence, imposed after his conviction of assault by means of force likely to produce great bodily injury.[35] This, he contended, was cruel and unusual punishment. Wingo had assaulted a slender 72-year-old man who walked with a cane. During daylight hours while he was walking in a park, the victim was knocked to the ground and repeatedly kicked in the head and torso. A bystander halted the attack.

The court noted at the outset that the same aggravated-assault statute "covers an extremely broad spectrum of culpable behavior" and would apply to a defendant whose offense was much less serious than Wingo's. The court then cited the first *Lynch* test, which requires analyzing the "nature of the offense and the offender with particular regard to the degree of danger both present to society." This, said the court, must be applied with regard to "the particular facts of the individual case." In *Lynch*, the determination was that under no circumstances could a second conviction for indecent exposure justify a potential life term. In contrast, the court stated in *Wingo* that the maximum penalty for aggravated assault "might be permissible in some circumstances but excessive in others." The court refused to make a square ruling on this issue in Wingo's particular case. It reasoned that

[i]f a statute proscribes a single narrowly delineated mode of behavior—as in Lynch—it is appropriate in considering the constitutionality of the penalty to look only to the maximum in order to determine whether under any circumstances the crime would justify the punishment. But this analytic proves inconclusive when applied to a statute regulating a broad variety of conduct, since by definition there is no single "offense" to measure against the subject penalty. Accordingly in this context a consideration of only the maximum is fruitless, leaving as our sole alternative a determination whether in light of the individual offense the actual penalty imposed is excessive.

Having rejected the defendant's argument that the penalty provision was void on its face, the court deferred any judicial determination of the possible disproportionality of Wingo's individual sentence, holding that such review would be inappropriate until after the Adult Authority had fixed Wingo's term. "The legislature is assumed to have intended that the statute be constitutionally applied," said the court, "and we thus interpret the penalty provision as presupposing that the Adult Authority would fix terms, within the statutory range, which are not disproportionate to the individual culpability of the offender." The court stated, however, that if the Adult Authority did not proceed promptly to set Wingo's term, then Wingo could pursue his challenge in the courts. In applying *Lynch*, the courts would then measure Wingo's particular conduct against the statutory maximum.

The *Wingo* decision's deferral to the Adult Authority seemed a major limitation on the substantive judicial review of penalties that *Lynch* and *Foss* had seemed to portend. Within six weeks of *Wingo*, the court clarified these three decisions, In *In re Rodriquez*,[36] Rodriquez had served 22 years of an indeterminate 1-year-to-life sentence for performing a sexual act upon a child.[37] The offense included no aggravating factors; the petitioner's background "reflected none of the characteristics associated with vicious criminality; his prison record had been exemplary."

The court began its analysis by examining two separate functions of the Adult Authority: (1) fixing terms (i.e., setting a maximum term lower than the life sentence authorized by statute) and (2) granting paroles. The authority's practice had been to fix terms only in conjunction with granting paroles. When a prisoner was given a tentative parole release date, his term was fixed in regard to the number of years to be served in prison and on parole. Typically, these terms were refixed at the maximum sentence if an offender's parole was revoked or a parole date rescinded.

Rodriquez had apparently never been deemed ready for parole. This was not because of prison infractions "but because the Authority cannot predict his future behavior, and because he is believed to lack the ability to care for himself and to conform to parole requirements except in a structured living situation with supervision." Thus, his term had never been set below the maximum—and he had spent the previous 16 of his 22 years' imprisonment at the maximum-security facility at San Quentin.

The court ordered his release. To reach this result, the court did not find it necessary to strike down the penalty statute as unconstitutional. It reasoned that the Adult Authority had a statutory—and, apparently, a constitutional—duty to fix terms without reference to a prisoner's "parole readiness." That term must be proportionate to the crime and "reflect the circumstances existing at the time of the offense." It must not be a sentence designed to fit the offender (instead of his crime), and it must not reflect judgments concerning his ability to return to the community and lead a law-abiding life.

The court found that the sentence Rodriquez had already served was clearly disproportionate to his crime, which "involved no violence and caused no physical harm to the victim."[38] Thus, the Adult Authority had failed in its responsibility to set a "constitutional maximum," and Rodriquez had to be released—not as a parolee, but as a prisoner unconditionally discharged.

These cases imposing procedural and substantive limitations on indeterminate sentencing reflect a growing judicial disenchantment with the indeterminate sentencing. Significant structural reform of sentencing is clearly on the horizon.

## VII/The Basic Question: Who Decides and When?

The central problem in criminal sentencing as it exists today is the diffusion of responsibility among organs of government that has resulted from the indeterminate sentence. No one person or institution really has responsibility for deciding the actual sentence.

The legislature sets a broad range, knowing that the judge and the parole board will really decide what sentence is appropriate in each case. The judge also imposes a range, knowing that the legislature has made the larger judgment and that the parole board will refine this. And the parole board, in deciding when this prisoner should actually be released, assumes that the broad moral judgments have already been made and all that is left is to administer the decision in accordance with its expertise.

This diffused responsibility probably has some practical effect in reducing sentences for offenses that are particularly unpopular. Who, for example, might be willing to take sole responsibility for releasing a pedophile or exhibitionist after six months? Certainly, not an elected official. However, such a decision could be made—though not without difficulty—under the present system of diffused responsibility. But this diffusion also has obvious and very serious drawbacks. It permits the system to operate on inertia, with no person or institution bearing the responsibility for making the fundamental moral decision: what is the *just* sentence for the typical perpetrator of a particular kind of crime, such as armed robbery?

The allocation of sentencing authority differs considerably, of course, from jurisdiction to jurisdiction and even within a given jurisdiction for different crimes. In some jurisdictions, the legislature has asserted the power to determine the sentence to be served, at least for certain crimes. Accordingly, mandatory sentences have been legislated for particular offenses. Examples are mandatory death penalty for felony-murder, mandatory one-year penalty for unauthorized possession of firearms, mandatory life imprisonment for trafficking in heroin, and mandatory five-year penalty for second crime involving use of a gun. In some jurisdictions, the legislature has empowered the trial courts to select from among a broad range of sentences; armed robbery, for example, might be punishable by any sentence up to 20 years. And in some jurisdictions, the legislature has limited the power of the trial court and vested real sentencing authority in the parole board. In such instances, the trial court imposes a statutory sentence from one day to life, and the parole board determines the actual duration of confinement. Obviously, all of this contributes to the enormous disparity in sentencing today in the United States.

What is urgently needed is a judgment concerning the relative amount of control that should properly be held by each particular institution. Clearly, this is a choice with important implications. It will determine to a large extent the process by which decisions will be made, what sentencing purposes will be emphasized at which points in an offender's involvement in the criminal process, and also to what extent it is possible to build flexibility, equality, predictability, or other values into the sentencing structure.

## SHIFT IN LOCUS AND TIMING

The legislatures, courts, and parole boards are the major elements in the criminal-sentencing system, and all have vital roles to play in the sentencing process. Other governmental bodies perforce play a limited role. The role of the executive branch is sharply curbed constitutionally and also by custom and practice. The President and the governors are not regarded as integral parts of the routine sentencing process; their intervention is properly limited to pardon and commutation in exceptional cases. The role of the jury in determining sentences within the legislatively specified range has been significantly curtailed in recent years and is now virtually nonexistent, except in certain special situations. The role of appellate courts is also rather limited. They sit to review abuses of discretion, and in some jurisdictions they are empowered to reduce (sometimes to increase) sentences that deviate substantially from some generally unarticulated norm.

In theory, the sentencing decision—whether to imprison and for how long—could be made at any stage in the process and by any of a number of decision makers. Indeed, it has been only very recently, with the emphasis on individualization of punishment, as we have noted earlier in this paper, that a greater role in determining the sentence has been allotted to the judge and the administrator. This has resulted in a shift in the locus of the sentencing decision, so that now the criminal defendant—and the general public—do not know what the sentence will be until after conviction. Indeed, as relatively indeterminate sentencing has emerged in most American jurisdictions, the real sentencing decision is often deferred until well after conviction while the defendant is in the midst of serving his sentence.

It is entirely possible for a just system to exist in which the sentence is determined before the trial—indeed, before the commission of the crime. In fact, most systems throughout history have had fixed sentences determined in advance of the crime and automatically imposed upon all persons convicted of committing the crime. It would, of course, be outrageous to impose the sentence before conviction, in the manner of the Red Queen in *Alice in Wonderland*—"first comes the sentence and only then the trial." But even that is done to some degree in all systems that authorize pretrial detention.

It is by no means clear that particular allocations of power will always result in the emphasis of particular goals or the development of certain types of decision-making processes. But it is possible to analyze the current behavior of the three major institutions in the criminal-sentencing system and to project what traits would likely become more or less influential in the sentencing process as more or less emphasis was placed upon each.

## THE JUDICIAL AND ADMINISTRATIVE MODELS

That we have become comfortable with judicial sentencing is perhaps in part because that decision seems intimately related to the trial process, which is controlled by the judge. The defendant is tried and found guilty; he is duly sentenced. Of course, this vision is seriously distorted in that the overwhelming majority of sentences are meted out after pleas of guilty. Nevertheless, until the recent controversy concerning sentencing disparity, judicially imposed sentences—even within a wide discretionary range—have been accepted as legitimate, so much so as to be immune from review for anything except exceeding the legislative maximum.

Why, in theory, a judge should be an appropriate sentencer is not altogether clear. Certainly, sentencing power is efficiently vested in him if it is to be exercised on the basis of events that occur around the time of the plea or the trial. Does the defendant seem repentant? Is he willing to assist the victim? Has he saved the state the expense of trial? These are some of the pertinent questions in this context.

Judicial sentencing today may thus serve largely judicial administrative goals rather than proper sentencing purposes. Ideally, a judicial-sentencing model would function according to fair, intelligible, and evenly applied standards or rules: it would be a truly "legal" model. Currently, this is not the case in view of widespread court-sanctioned, court-encouraged plea bargaining—a system that functions with no valid, consistent reference to the goals of isolating, punishing, or rehabilitating the individual offender for a particular offense.

In still another way, administrative sentencing likewise operates under strong pressures to serve functions that are probably not major or even proper goals of a just sentencing system. The parole board's main strength is that it is supposed to be composed of independent experts. In fact, the parole board is heavily, even wholly, dependent upon institutional staff members for information concerning offenders who are eligible for release. The parole board thus is likely to become a sort of prison disciplinary agency, the rationale being that good prisoners are likely to be good citizens on the outside.

The enormous caseload that most boards must handle means that parole "processing" of offenders is just that. Parole-release is meant to be a personal process, with lengthy face-to-face interviews and a detailed evaluation of the offender's progress and prognosis. But in the great bulk of cases, nothing could be farther from reality. Instead of serving the inmate's rehabilitative needs, the administrative model may actually undermine such goals because it operates in such a haphazard manner.

## WEAKNESSES AND STRENGTHS OF THE LEGISLATURE

Though democratic theory allocates to the legislature the power to make fundamental judgments of policy, it also recognizes that the representative nature of that body necessitates safeguards against its susceptibility to popular passions and pressures. This same quality makes that body quite inept at the sustained, disciplined effort required to elaborate a rational, just sentencing system. First, there is the continuing pressure of other business—tasks that the general public views as of higher priority than merely tinkering with a set of sanctions that directly affects only a tiny minority of citizens. Second, there are the considerable pressures to ignore this tiny minority as a valid constituency and to represent the interests of only the law-abiding voter.

Since criminals are not a vocal constituency, legislatures have responded to the demand of the victims, both past and prospective, for harsher punishments. It has been difficult for legislators to oppose legislation imposing outrageously harsh penalties on sex offenders and drug offenders. It has also been difficult to resist the pressures of economic institutions, such as banks and department stores, to increase the penalties for check forgery, shoplifting, and other crimes affecting vested financial interests. Thus, the legislature would seem most likely to make sentencing judgments that further the purposes of isolation and punishment. Rehabilitation apparently occupies a somewhat ambiguous niche in the legislative hierarchy of values. Its rank may be dependent on financial considerations. Do diversion and community programs cost substantially less than full prosecution and incarceration? If so, they earn votes. Don't in-prison educational and vocational training for already incarcerated offenders cost substantially more than simple custodial maintenance? If so, such programs have extraordinary difficulty competing for tax dollars. In such ways is the legislator hemmed in by electoral pressures and fiscal priorities.

It is argued, therefore, that trial judges and parole boards are better able to resist these passions and pressures in deciding on appropriate sentences for particular crimes and criminals. In other words, sentences would be harsher for at least certain categories of crimes and criminals if more power over sentencing were exercised by legislatures rather than by courts or parole boards.

The available evidence does not bear out that assertion. Indeed, as noted earlier in this paper, the introduction of indeterminate sentencing has coincided with a sharp increase in the confinement statutorily authorized for particular crimes and in the judicial maxima actually imposed.[1] There is also evidence, albeit inconclusive, that prisoners incarcerated under indeterminate-sentencing laws serve longer terms of imprisonment than prisoners convicted of comparable crimes in jurisdictions using relatively fixed sentences. In 1927, one commentator summarized the evidence as follows:

> While parole was originally conceived of as a means of shortening the period of incarceration of deserving inmates who could be trusted with conditional freedom, it has become, in actual practice, a mechanism by which

something is added on to prison sentences. The universal conclusion of studies of time served in prison under indeterminate sentence laws and time served under the old definite sentence laws in the same jurisdictions has been that the indeterminate sentences have very materially increased the time served within the walls.[2]

Said another scholar 31 years later: "It is clear that no matter what other factors govern sentence length, the inevitable result of the indeterminate sentence is that sentences of over five years will strongly predominate; and in a definite sentence state sentences of under five years will strongly predominate."[3]

Are these differences causally related? At least one distinguished observer attributes the differences to the impact of other factors, including the higher volume of crime in many of the states with indeterminate-sentence laws.[4] In sum, it is difficult to test the hypothesis that legislatures, in general, would impose harsher fixed sentences than those imposed by the courts and parole boards today.

Beyond this lies an even more profound consideration. The questions of justice and policy embodied in the sentencing decision involve the relative seriousness of crimes and the level of punishment appropriate for each crime and/or type of criminal—questions of enormous gravity both for individuals and for society. Democratic theory would seem to dictate that such important decisions concerning human liberty should be made by the most representative elected body. There can be no doubt that, of the three bodies involved in the criminal-sentencing system, the legislature is more representative than the trial court (even when nominally elected) or the parole board. The legislative process, whatever its shortcomings, is the most open; debates are public, votes are recorded, and anyone may present an opinion to a representative for his consideration.

Democratic theory also imposes constraints upon the legislative role in sentencing. The ex post facto and bill of attainder clauses of the Constitution limit the role of the legislature in sentencing decisions; it may not make individual sentencing determinations about past crimes, and it may make only general sentencing determinations about future crimes. And the Constitution limits the degree of punishments authorized to those which are not cruel and unusual (or disproportionate or whatever other formulation appears in the relevant state constitution).

It is clear that no democratic society would ever leave it to judges, administrators, or experts to decide which acts should constitute crimes. That decision is quintessentially legislative, involving, as it does, fundamental questions of policy. Likewise, it should not be left to judges, administrators, or experts to determine the bases on which criminal offenders in a democratic society should be deprived lawfully of their freedom.

# Appendix to the Background Paper

## Indeterminate Versus Determinate Sentencing

To the extent a sentence is fixed, a judge imposes it before the defendant has begun to serve it; whereas, to the extent a sentence is indeterminate, an administrative agency imposes it while it is being served. These differences produce several important effects, three of which seem most significant.

1. *To the extent that a judge has the power to determine the sentence at trial, he is more likely to consider the defendant's conduct at the trial and prior thereto.*

Thus, judicial sentencing focuses on such factors as whether the defendant pleaded guilty or not guilty, whether he cooperated with the prosecutor, and whether he committed perjury at the trial. To the extent that an administrative agency has the power to determine the sentence while the defendant is serving it, an agency is more likely to consider the defendant's conduct in prison, focusing on such factors as the prisoner's disciplinary record and his general cooperativeness as a prisoner.

The point in the process at which the sentence is actually determined is probably not the only reason for this difference. Being lawyers who identify more with the prosecution function in the criminal process, judges naturally use their power more in the service of that aspect of the process (by rewarding pleas of guilty and cooperation with the prosecutor). Members of the parole board, on the other hand, generally identify more closely with the correction function of the process and use their power more in the service of that aspect of the process (by rewarding prison cooperation and good behavior).

2.  *To the extent that a sentence is determined later rather than earlier in the process, the sentencing authority naturally will look more to the future than to the past.*

The later the sentencing takes place, the closer it is in time to release. There is more information about release plans, job prospects, current mental condition, and prisoner attitude. The crime itself is further in the past, and community hostility (except for notorious crimes) is less likely to be an overriding consideration. Put in practical terms, the judge sentencing early in the process is more likely to ask himself how the community will react if the sentence is disproportionate to the past crime, whereas the agency sentencing later in the process is likely to ask itself how the community would react if the released prisoner were to recidivate. (These considerations merge, of course, when the sentencing judge is deciding whether to impose a prison sentence at all.) Thus, predictive considerations, though they undoubtedly enter into all sentencing decisions no matter by whom or when they are made, may play a greater role in indeterminate sentencing than in fixed sentencing.

3.  *To the extent that a sentence is imposed by a judge at the close of trial, it is far more amenable to appellate challenge and review than if it were determined later by a board.*

Defendants are generally represented by counsel at the time of judicial sentencing but not while they are serving an indeterminate sentence. (A case can be made for the right to counsel at all times before the sentence is actually decided upon by the board, but that is not the current law.) A related reason is that the appeal from conviction provides a convenient vehicle to which to attach a sentencing challenge; it is far more difficult to bring an action challenging an ongoing sentence whose duration has not yet been determined. However, recent decisions, notably *In re Lynch,* discussed in Chapter VI, may make it easier to challenge ongoing sentences.

Certain final observations about indeterminate versus determinate sentencing in general also ought to be made.

It should be noted that the question of sentencing discretion transcends that of the indeterminate sentence; it concerns also the range of sentences available to trial judges. The problem of sentencing discretion would still remain if judges were required to fix a wholly determinate sentence, as long as they were empowered to select that sentence from a wide range of legislatively authorized alternatives. To take an extreme case, consider a statute that permitted the sentencing judge to select any term of years between 1 and 50 as the appropriate sentence for armed robbery but required him to fix the sentence with precision at the time of imposition (e.g., 18 years, without the possibility of parole). Under such a sentencing scheme, no discretion would be vested in an administrative agency, but extremely broad discretion would be vested in the judge. One of the avowed purposes of the relatively indeterminate sentence is to counteract the enormous disparities in sentences imposed by different judges for similar offenses. The theory is that a professional agency acting collectively will produce less disparity than individual judges.

It should be remembered that the concept of indeterminacy is not applicable exclusively to punitive criminal sentences. Other kinds of involuntary confinement that do not bear punitive labels—such as commitment of the insane, addicts, juvenile delinquents, defective delinquents, and sexual psychopaths—are typically indeterminate. Indeed, they tend to be even more indeterminate than criminal sentences. Commitments of the mentally ill, sexual psychopaths, and defective delinquents are wholly indeterminate as a general rule. "Nonpunitive" confinements of juveniles and addicts usually have upper time limits, but administrative boards have discretion to determine the actual duration of the confinement within these limits.

Finally, almost all sentences can be shortened by executive clemency, pardon, and the like. In this sense, all sentences may be regarded as indeterminate. But executive intervention theoretically is reserved for special situations; therefore, it has not been considered in this paper. Nor has the paper considered mandatory good-time provisions, which automatically reduce a given sentence by a certain amount if the prisoner complies with prison rules. While large elements of discretion certainly enter into good-time decisions, such decisions are not (at least theoretically) part of the indeterminate-sentence structure.

They did, however, play an important role in the early history of what ultimately evolved into the indeterminate sentence.

# Notes

## Chapter I

[1]This is not to deny the importance of other, nonutilitarian purposes of the criminal sentence (see N.8). Nor is it to deny the overall centrality of considerations of justice, equity, and proportionality in determining the degree of punishment. See A. von Hirsch, *Doing Justice: The Choice of Punishments*, Report of the Committee for the Study of Incarceration (New York: Hill and Wang, 1976), chap. XII.

[2]Isolation is sometimes referred to as "incapacitation," but the latter term is inaccurate because the prisoner often retains the capacity to commit further crimes while in prison. Only the locus and victim group are changed; the crimes are now directed at other prisoners, guards, or—on occasion—visitors. Some prisoners—such as organized crime bosses—may be able to continue to direct their crimes against the outside population even while serving a sentence of imprisonment. "Incapacitation" is more accurately used to describe mechanisms designed directly to reduce the convicted person's capacity to commit certain crimes. Such mechanisms historically have included castration, removal of limbs, and occupational disqualifications.

[3]*Cross v. Harris*, 418 F.2d 1095, 1110 (D. C. Cir. 1969) with J. Burger concurring and dissenting in part.

[4]For example, even if it were true that many, most, or virtually all of those currently isolated would have committed serious crimes if they had remained free during their periods of isolation, that would still not tell us how many crimes were ultimately prevented. It may well be that certain criminals "store up" certain kinds of crimes; that is, if a criminal would have committed three serious crimes each year, it does not necessarily follow that his isolation for two years would have the net effect of preventing six crimes; it may well be that, upon his release, he will commit four crimes rather than three during his first two years out, thus resulting in a net prevention of only four crimes.

[5]Assume 1,000 prisoners, 900 of whom would have averaged 3 serious crimes during their terms of imprisonment; 2,700 serious crimes would thus have been "prevented." But if there were 27,000 serious crimes committed by others during that same period, then only 10 percent of serious crimes would directly have been prevented by isolating the 1,000 persons.

[6]See A. Dershowitz, "Preventing Preventive Detention," *New York Review of Books* (March 13, 1969), p. 27.

[7]See Dershowitz, "Preventive Confinement: A Suggested Framework for Constitutional Analysis," *Texas Law Review*, 51 (1973):1277, 1283–1288.

[8]See R. Saleilles, *The Individualization of Punishment*, translated from the 2nd French edition by R. Szold Jastrow (Boston: Little, Brown, 1911), p. 186.

[9]F. E. Zimring and G. J. Hawkins, *Deterrents: The Legal Threat in Crime Control* (Chicago: University of Chicago Press, 1973).

[10]Compare Sellin with Ehrlich. The article was published in *Law in the United States in Social and Technological Revolution*, ed. J. N. Hazard and W. J. Wagner (Brussels: American Association for the Comparative Study of Law, 1974).

[11]"The Penal Law is a Categorical Imperative; and woe unto him who creeps through the serpent-windings of Utilitarianism to discover some advantage that may discharge him from the Justice of Punishment. ..." Kant, *Philosophy of Law*, Hastie translation (Edinburgh: 1887), pp. 195–196.

[12]See, for example, G. Lombroso Ferrero, *Criminal Man, According to the Classification of Cesare Lombroso* (New York: G. P. Putnam, 1911).

[13]See Dershowitz, "Indeterminate Sentencing as a Mechanism of Preventive Confinement," in *Law in the United States in Social and Technological Revolution*.

[14]Justice is a two-edged sword. It would be unjust to sentence a convicted purse snatcher to an unduly long prison term (leaving for a moment the difficult question of how long is too long); it would also be unjust to sentence a convicted murderer to an unduly minor punishment.

[15]See von Hirsch, *Doing Justice*.

[16]R. Martison, "What Works?—Questions and Answers about Prison Reform," *The Public Interest*, 22 (Spring 1974). Martison's review includes rehabilitation programs outside the prison walls—probation and parole techniques—but, for all these, his conclusion is the same.

[17]There is, of course, some circularity inherent in all discussions of sentencing mechanisms, since each mechanism depends—to some degree—on assumed justifications relating to other mechanisms.

[18]There still is room for questioning the goals sought through rehabilitation, even voluntary rehabilitation. See "South Africa Plans Rehabilitation Centers for Blacks Violating Racial Laws," *New York Times* (July 20, 1975), p. 4, col. 1.

[19]This formulation deliberately leaves out the entire issue of whether dangerous persons who have not been convicted may be preventively confined.

[20]That such a system is not unthinkable is evidenced by the fact that it was proposed by early advocates for indeterminate sentencing: "No man be imprisoned unless it is clear that his freedom is dangerous to others, and that when once imprisoned, no man be free until the danger has ceased." C. T. Lewis, "The Indeterminate Sentence," *Yale Law Journal*, 9 (1899): 17.

[21]A just system of confinement would mandate release as soon as the standard of dangerousness was no longer met or as soon as the confinement became disproportionate to the past crime and the predicted harm, whichever came earlier. See Dershowitz, "Indeterminate Confinement: Letting the Therapy Fit the Harm," *University of Pennsylvania Law Review*, 123 (1974):297.

# Chapter II

[1]D. Rothman, *The Discovery of the Asylum: Social Order and Disorder in the New Republic* (Boston: Little, Brown, 1971). See also W. L. Morse et al., eds., *The Attorney General's Survey of Release Procedures,* vol. 1, *Digest of Laws;* vol. 2, *Probation;* vol. 3, *Pardon;* vol. 4, *Parole;* vol. 5, *Prisons.* Volumes 1–4 were published by the U.S. Government Printing Office, Washington, D.C., 1939. Volume 5 was published by Federal Prison Industries, Inc., Press, 1940. This work is hereinafter referred to as *Release Procedures.*

[2]H. B. Gill, "A New Prison Discipline: Implementing the Declaration of Principles of 1870," *Federal Probation,* 34 (June 1970):29.

# Chapter III

[1]Several colonies had "bounty systems" for bringing property offenders to justice: victims who apprehended and prosecuted the perpetrators received triple restitution if there was a conviction. For example, Chap. 18 of the 1736–37 Province Laws for Massachusetts, provided that

> if any person who stands convict upon record, either before a justice of the peace, or in any court of general sessions of the peace within this province, for stealing, shall after that presume to steal any money, goods or chattels, to the value of forty shillings lawful money, and be thereof convict by due course of law, before the court of assize and general goal delivery, holden within any of the count(ie)(y)s of this province, he or they for such offence, shall, besides paying treble the value of such money, goods or chattles so stolen, to the party injured, together with costs and charges of prosecution, be set(t) upon the gallows for the space of one hour, with a rope around his neck, and one end thereof cast over the gallows, and be severely whipt not exceeding thirty stripes.

[2]For example, the 1676 Duke of Yorke's Laws (Pennsylvania) provided that

> [i]f any person whatsoever shall kindle any fire in the woods or Grounds lying in Common, or in his own Grounds so as the same shall runne into any Corne Grounds or Enclosures of his Neighboures, he shall be Lyable to pay all Damage; of whatsoever Sort, and half so much more for a fine; or if not able to pay the Court shall Adjudge the Person guilty of Corporal punishment not exceeding twenty Stripes, or do Service to Expiate the Crime.

See, generally, A. M. Earle, *Curious Punishments of Bygone Days* (1972), cited in D. Fogel, *"We Are the Living Proof"*: The Justice Model for Corrections (Cincinnati: W. H. Anderson, 1975), pp. 7–9.

[3]The preamble to the Massachusetts statute cited supra at n.1 reasoned

[w]hereas the punishments already provided by law against stealing have proved ineffectual, and even those that have suffered the penalty in such cases have been so bold and hardy as to perpetrate their wickedness a second and even a third time; for the more effectual preventing whereof,—

the stiffer penalty structure was enacted. In addition to the second-offender provision cited at n.1, the third-offender section dictated

[t]hat if any person convicted of a second theft, in a manner as aforesaid, shall presume a third time to steal any money, goods or chatt(e)1(e)s, to the value of three pounds lawful money, and be therof convict by due course of law, he shall be adjudged to suffer the pains of death without benefit of clergy.

[4]*Charter and Laws of Pennsylvania,* 1682–1700, p. 121.
[5]The 1750 "rioting assembly" law in Massachusetts

[p]rovided always . . . that where there shall appear any circumstances to mitigate or alleviate any of the offenses against this act, in the judgment of the court before which such offense shall be tried, it shall and may be lawful for the judges of such court to abate the whole of the punishment of whipping or such part thereof as they shall judge proper (Province Laws of 1750, chap. 17, sec. 5).

[6]Typically, the court was instructed to calibrate its sentence "according to the nature and aggravation of the offense." The Massachusetts "maiming" statute, Chap. 123, Sec. 4, of the Acts of 1804, covered a wide variety of behavior and directed the justices to adjust their punishments to fit this standard:

[I]f any person, with set purpose and aforethought Malice, or intention to maim or disfigure, shall unlawfully cut out or disable the tongue, put out an Eye, cut off an Ear, slit the Nose, or cut off the Nose or lip, or Cut off or disable a limb or member of any person, every such offender, and every person privy to the intent aforesaid, who shall be present, aiding and abetting in the Commission of such offence, or not being present, shall have Counselled, hired or procured the same to be done, upon due conviction thereof in the Supreme Judicial Court, shall be punished by Solitary imprisonment, for such term, not exceeding ten Years, commencing from the expiration of such solitary imprisonment, as the Justices of the said Court, before whom the Conviction may be shall sentence and order, according to the nature and aggravation of the offence.

[7]Cesare Beccaria, *On Crimes and Punishments*, trans. H. Paolucci (Indianapolis: Bobbs-Merrill, 1963), pp. 58, 94, quoted in Rothman, op. cit., p. 58.
[8]See O. F. Lewis, *The Development of American Prisons and Prison Customs, 1776–1845* (Albany: Prison Association of New York, 1922), pp. 16–24, cited in *Release Procedures*, vol. 5, p. 2.

⁹Some states did, however, have good-time laws that allowed an inmate to earn a set amount of sentence reduction through good behavior in prison. New York enacted the first good-time law in 1817: it allowed a first-term inmate with a sentence of less than five years to shorten his sentence by one-fourth. The law, however, was apparently not used. E. H. Sutherland, *Criminology* (Philadelphia: J. B. Lippincott, 1924) pp. 508–509. A history of good-time enactments is included in *Release Procedures,* vol. 4, pp. 495–511.
¹⁰See *Laws of New York* (1801), chap. 58.
¹¹See Rothman, op. cit., pp. 247–249.
¹²Quoted in *Release Procedures,* vol. 4, p. 17.

## Chapter IV

¹*Transactions of the National Congress on Prisons and Reformatory Discipline* (Albany, N.Y.: American Correctional Association, 1871), reprinted by the American Correctional Association, Weed and Parsons, eds. (1970), cited in Fogel, op. cit., p. 32.
²Ibid.
³Z. Brockway, *Fifty Years of Prison Service* (N.Y.: Charities Publication Committee, 1912), p. 401.
⁴Ibid., p. 391.
⁵C. Lewis, "The Indeterminate Sentence," p. 17.
⁶Ibid.
⁷Ibid., p. 24.
⁸Ibid.
⁹E. Lindsey, "Historical Sketch of the Indeterminate Sentence and Parole System," *Journal of Criminal Law and Criminology,* 16 (1925):18.
¹⁰Ibid., p. 21.
¹¹Ibid., p. 22.
¹²In 1922, 44 states, the territory of Hawaii, and the federal government had parole systems; 37 of these had some form of indeterminate sentencing; only 4 states were without either. Lindsey, op. cit., pp. 9, 39, 58, 69. Here are the 13 forms of indeterminate sentence catalogued by Lindsey:

1. The sentence indefinite in form but the maximum period of detention limited by the Act to the maximum prescribed by law for the offense of which the prisoner was convicted. This is the form adopted in the case of the reformatories generally, wherever located, and is patterned after the Elmira Act.
2. The sentence indefinite in form but with both maximum and minimum period of detention limited by the Act to the maximum and minimum prescribed by law for the offense of which convicted. This form was adopted in Ohio, Michigan, Minnesota, and Illinois.
3. A maximum and minimum period to be fixed by the court in the sentence but with the provision in the Act that the maximum shall not exceed the maximum prescribed by law for the offense. New York.

4. The court to fix the maximum and minimum period of detention in the sentence but with the provision in the Act that the maximum shall not exceed the maximum prescribed by law for the offense and the minimum shall not be less than two and one-half years. Massachusetts.

5. The court to name the maximum and minimum period of detention in the sentence, which shall be the maximum and minimum prescribed by law for the offense. The Indiana Act.

6. A maximum and minimum term to be fixed by the court in the sentence which must be within the maximum and minimum terms prescribed by the law for the offense of which the prisoner was convicted. This form first appeared in the Kansas Act and was adopted also by New Hampshire, New Mexico, Kentucky, Wyoming, Washington and the New York Act of 1909.

7. A maximum and minimum term to be fixed by the court in the sentence; the maximum shall be the maximum prescribed by law for the offense and not more than one-half the maximum. Idaho.

8. A maximum term to be fixed by the court in the sentence which shall not exceed the maximum prescribed by statute for the offense. This form was adopted in Minnesota and Orgeon.

9. The court to fix in the sentence a minimum term which shall be the minimum prescribed by statute for the offense and a maximum term which shall be the time fixed by the jury in its verdict. Adopted in Texas.

10. The court to fix in the sentence a maximum term which shall be the maximum prescribed by statute for the offense and a minimum which shall not be less than one year nor more than one-half the maximum. New Jersey.

11. The court to fix in the sentence a maximum term which shall not exceed the maximum prescribed by statute for the offense and a minimum term which shall be the minimum prescribed by statute for the offense. Maine.

12. The court to fix in the sentence a minimum term within the limits prescribed by statute for the offense, but no prisoner to be detained beyond the maximum prescribed by statute for the offense. Ohio.

13. The jury to fix a maximum and minimum in its verdict within the maximum and minimum prescribed by statute for the offense. Georgia.

[13]H. E. Barnes, *The Evolution of Penology in Pennsylvania: A Study in American Social History* (Indianapolis: Bobbs Merrill, 1927).

[14]R. Gault, "The Parole System as a Means of Protection," in *Journal of Criminal Law and Criminology,* 5 (1915):799, 806.

[15]U.S. Department of Justice, Law Enforcement Assistance Administration, National Criminal Justice Information and Statistics Service, *Prisoners in State and Federal Institutions on December 31, 1971, 1972, and 1973* (Washington, D.C.: U.S. Government Printing Office, 1975), p. 25.

[16]In 1966, of 88,000 felony releases, 61 percent were paroled, 5 percent obtained another type of conditional release, and 34 percent were discharged. Federal Bureau of Prisons, *National Prisoner Statistics: Prisoners in State and Federal Institutions for Adult Felons, 1966* (Washington, D.C.: Fed-

eral Bureau of Prisons, 1968), p. 43. In 1970, of 83,000 felony releases, 72 percent were paroled, 9 percent obtained another type of conditional release, and 19 percent were discharged. Federal Bureau of Prisons, *National Prisoner Statistics: Prisoners in State and Federal Institutions for Adult Felons, 1970* (Washington, D.C.: Federal Bureau of Prisons, 1970), p. 43. Both of these statistical studies are cited in the National Advisory Commission on Criminal Justice Standards and Goals, *Corrections* (Washington, D.C.: U.S. Government Printing Office, 1973), p. 389. The trend, then, is clear; indeed, given the overcrowding in many prisons, it would not be surprising that parole boards reacted to felt pressures to release more prisoners if only to make space for new ones.

[17]Compare *Leach v. United States*, 334 F.2d 945 (D.C. Cir. 1964), with *Lake v. Cameron*, 364 F.2d 657 (D.C. Cir. 1966).

[18]See also Barnes, op. cit., p. 193.

[19]F. P. Mihm, "A Re-examination of the Validity of Our Sex Psychopath Statutes in the Light of Recent Appeal Cases and Experience," in *Journal of Criminal Law and Criminology,* 44(1954):716, 718.

[20]"There is considerable evidence, mainly in the form of testimony from prisoners and ex-prisoners of various California prisons, that indefinite sentences are one of the most painful aspects of prison life." American Friends Service Committee, *Struggle for Justice: A Report on Crime and Punishment in America* (New York: Hill and Wang, 1971), p. 93. See also J. Mitford, *Kind and Usual Punishment: The Prisoner Business* (New York: Knopf, 1973), p. 87.

*The Official Report of the New York State Special Commission on Attica* (1972) found that "the operation of the parole system was a primary source of tension and bitterness within the walls" (p. 93).

The prisoner's refusal to appreciate the beneficence of the rehabilitative purpose purportedly underlying indeterminate sentencing has often led to a charade in which the prison-wise criminal seeks to avoid an indeterminate sentence by demonstrating that he is incorrigible and not amenable to rehabilitation. For a striking example of this phenomenon, see *People v. Jemmot*, 50 Misc. 2d 640, 271 N.Y.S. 2d 41 *rev'd*, 26 App. Div. 2d 937, 274 N.Y.S. 2d 466 (1966).

[21]The 1960s saw a "prisoners' rights" movement develop, partly as an outgrowth of the civil rights and war resistance movements, which had resulted in the imprisonment of more middle-class persons closer to the sources of power, influence, and publicity than was the "core" population of prisons.

[22]See, for example, N. Morris, "The Future of Imprisonment: Toward a Punitive Philosophy," *Michigan Law Review,* 72 (1974):1161, 1164–73. ("Despite the weight of authority supporting the principle of dangerousness, it must be rejected because it presupposes a capacity to predict quite beyond our present or foreseeable technical ability" [p. 1167].)

See, generally, B. L. Diamond, "The Psychiatric Prediction of Dangerousness," *University of Pennsylvania Law Review,* 123 (1974):439; von Hirsch, "Predictions of Criminal Conduct and Preventive Confinement of Convicted Persons," *Buffalo Law Review*, 21 (1972):717; Dershowitz, "Psychiatry and the Legal Process," *Journal of the American Judicature Society,* 51 (1968):370, 376–77.

[23]See, for example, Martison, op. cit.; J. Conrad, *Crime and Its Correction: An International Survey of Attitudes and Practices* (London: Tavistock, 1965); G.

Kassebaum et al., *Prison Treatment and Parole Survival: An Empirical Assessment* (New York: Wiley, 1970), pp. 307–313; F. A. Allen, "Criminal Justice, Legal Values and the Rehabilitative Ideal," *Journal of Criminal Law, Criminology, and Police Science,* 50 (1959):226; J. Andanaes, "The General Preventive Effects of Punishment," *University of Pennsylvania Law Review,* 114 (1966):949, 973–974; J. Robison and G. Smith, "The Effectiveness of Correctional Programs," *Crime and Delinquency,* 17 (1971):67.

[24]American Friends Service Committee, op. cit., see n. 20.

[25]Ibid., p. 76.

[26]Ibid.

[27]Ibid., p. 78. To the extent that this report suggests that preventive detention is a recent phenomenon, it is wrong. See Dershowitz, "The Origins of Preventive Confinement in Anglo-American Law," *University of Cincinnati Law Review,* 43 (1974):1.

[28]Mitford, op. cit., p. 81, see n. 9.

[29]Ibid., p. 83.

[30]Ibid., p. 87.

[31]"A prestigious and influential scholarly product, the Model Penal Code, provides for broadly indeterminate sentences. A number of state legislatures, including several influenced by the Model Penal Code have opted for indeterminacy in recent revisions of their laws." M. Frankel, *Criminal Sentences—Law without Order* (New York: Hill and Wang, 1972), p. 88.

[32]Ibid. Judge Frankel acknowledges the impact of prisoners' complaints on resisting the trend toward indeterminacy: "Until the last couple of years, the trend toward indeterminate sentencing has seemed irresistible. Just recently, from the prisons and elsewhere, some voices of dissent have been heard."

[33]Ibid., p. 98.

[34]Ibid., p. 100. "It is easy to err on the side of overcaution, resolving doubts in favor of confinement. But while that appears in fact to have happened on a large scale, nobody worth listening to commends it as a happy course for a civilized society."

## Chapter V

[1]American Friends Service Committee, op. cit., p. 96.

[2]U.S. Department of Justice, Federal Bureau of Prisons, *Federal Bureau of Prisons Statistical Report: Fiscal Years 1971 and 1972* (Washington, D.C.: U.S. Bureau of Prisons), pp. 152–153. However, only 27 convicted extortionists were released in 1971–72.

[3]U.S. Department of Justice, Federal Bureau of Prisons, *National Prisoner Statistics: State Prisoners, Admissions and Releases, 1970* (Washington, D.C.: U.S. Bureau of Prisons), pp. 45, 47–81. The data is charted and reproduced in National Advisory Commission on Criminal Justice Standards and Goals, op. cit., p. 144.

[4]National Advisory Commission on Criminal Justice Standards and Goals, op. cit., p. 145. The text points out, for example, that "since the figures deal only with offenders sentenced to confinement, a State which has an active probation system and confines only the most recalcitrant offenders could be expected to show longer sentences than a State which has only a few

community-based programs and imprisons almost all convicted offenders." This particular explanation of what might otherwise be misleading comparisions actually demonstrates another type of disparity.

⁵A. Partridge and W. Eldridge, eds., *The Second Circuit Sentencing Study: A Report to the Judges of the Second Circuit* (Washington, D.C.: Federal Judicial Center, 1974).

⁶For this judge's views on the problem of sentencing disparity, see C. B. Motley, "Law and Order and the Criminal Justice System," *Journal of Criminal Law and Criminology*, 64 (1973):259, 263–269.

⁷L. Cargan and M. Coates, "The Indeterminate Sentence and Judicial Bias," *Crimes and Delinquency*, 19 (1974):144.

⁸L. J. Toliver et al., *Sentencing and the Law and Order Syndrome in South Carolina* (St. Paul, Minn.: West Publishing Co., 1974).

⁹Ibid., p. 83.

¹⁰*Report of the National Institute for Law Enforcement and Criminal Justice*, reprinted in part IV of *Reform of the Federal Criminal Laws, Hearings before the Subcommittee on Criminal Laws and Procedures of the Senate Committee on the Judiciary*, 92d Cong., 2d sess. 3896–3912, and reprinted in *New York State Bar Journal*, 45 (1973):163.

¹¹See, for example, E. Green, *Judicial Attitudes in Sentencing* (London: Macmillan, 1961), pp. 8–20; H. Mannheim, "Some Aspects of Judicial Sentencing Policy," *Yale Law Journal*, 67 (1958):961; J. Hogarth, *Sentencing as a Human Process* (Toronto: University of Toronto Press, 1971), pp. 6–12; M. Hindelang, "Equality Under Law," *Journal of Criminal Law, Criminology and Police Science*, 60 (1969):306.

¹²For an examination of the possible influence of socioeconomic status, age, and sex, in addition to race, on sentencing decisions, see J. Hagan, "Extra-Legal Attributory and Criminal Sentencing: An Assessment of Sociological Viewpoint," *Law and Society Review*, 8 (1974):357.

  For discussions of the sentencing relevance of individual judges' characteristics and biases, see S. Nagel, "Ethnic Affiliations and Judicial Propensities," *Journal of Politics*, 24 (1962):92; W. Gaylin, *Partial Justice: A Study of Bias in Sentencing* (New York: Knopf, 1974); Hogarth, op. cit.

¹³See, for example, T. Hawkinson, "Conviction and Sentencing in the Fourth Judicial District of Nebraska: The Effect of Pre-Trial Release, Race and Prior Arrest on Conviction and Sentencing," *Creighton Law Review*, 8 (1975):923; H. A. Bullock, "Significance of the Racial Factor in the Length of Prison Sentence," *Journal of Criminal Law, Criminology and Police Science*, 52 (1961):411; E. Green, "Inter- and Intra-racial Crime Relative to Sentencing," ibid., 55 (1964):348; M. E. Wolfgang et al., "Comparison of the Executed and the Commuted among Admissions to Death Row," ibid., 53 (1962):301; T. Sellin, "Race Prejudice in the Administration of Justice," *American Journal of Sociology*, 41(1935):212; D. H. Parrington, "The Incidence of the Death Penalty for Rape in Virginia," *Washington and Lee Law Review*, 22 (1965):43; D. M. Petersen and P. C. Friday, "Early Release from Incarceration: Race as a Factor in the Use of 'Shock Probation,'" *Journal of Criminal Law and Criminology*, 66 (1975):79.

¹⁴L. P. Tiffany et al., "A Statistical Analysis of Sentencing in Federal Courts: Defendants Convicted after Trial, 1967–1968," *Journal of Legal Studies*, 4 (1975):369.

¹⁵Ibid., p. 379. In general, the authors concluded that when the crime is perceived as being less serious, individual factors such as prior record seem

to be given relatively more weight than when the crime is more serious—there uniformity ("let the punishment fit the crime") seems to be more important.

[16]Ibid., p. 387. In fact, the report states, "There is something about the combination of bench trial and type of lawyer that has a powerful effect on sentencing." When the authors controlled for other variables, they found that, after bench trial, the "weighted sentence scale" was 8.2 with retained lawyers and 12.7 with appointed lawyers.

[17]Ibid., pp. 388–390.

[18]"Southern District of New York Sentencing Study," Mimeograph dated January 10, 1973, reprinted in *New York State Bar Journal,* 45 (1973):163.

[19]For other studies of sentencing within a particular jurisdiction, see Comment, "Discretion in Felony Sentencing—A Study of Influencing Factors," *Washington Law Review,* 48 (1973):857, and Note, "Sentencing Patterns in the Northern District of Alabama: An Empirical Study," *Cumberland Samford Law Review,* 5 (1974):88. The author of the former study concludes (p. 878) that race is significant. The previous criminal record of the offender is much more important than the nature of the current crime. Factors unrelated to the defendant's culpability or rehabilitation potential have great impact on the sentence. Factors from the judge's background such as education and length of legal practice are extremely important in accounting for particular sentences.

The author of the latter study, although finding apparent evidence of disparity, nevertheless seems to feel that "individualization and flexibility" operated to set appropriate sentencing on a "case by case basis": "Each sentence is to be determined with its peculiar facts and circumstances in mind" (p. 103). The actual—and appropriate variables—are not canvassed.

## Chapter VI

[1]*In re Gault,* 387, U.S. 1, 70 (1967), J. Harlan concurring and dissenting.

[2]See also the opinions of Chief Judge Bazelon in *Bolton v. Harris,* 395 F.2d 642 (D.C. Cir. 1968)—(persons found not guilty by reason of insanity entitled to judicial hearing prior to civil commitment), and *Millard v. Cameron,* 373 F.2d 468 (D.C. Cir. 1966)—(procedural safeguards prior to civil commitment under sexual-psychopath statute.

[3]386 U.S. 605 (1967).

[4]Ibid., 607.

[5]Ibid.

[6]Ibid., 608–609.

[7]Ibid., 606.

[8]Ibid., 608–610.

[9]58 N.J. 238, 277 A.2d 193 (1971).

[10]Ibid., at 239, 277 A.2d at 193. "His period of confinement was indeterminate, to continue until the appropriate authority decided that he should be paroled though not beyond the maximum provided by law with respect to an adult."

[11]Ibid., 240, 277 A. 2d at 194.

[12]Ibid., 241, 277 A.2d at 194.

[13]Ibid., 249–250, 277 A.2d at 1991.

[14]E. Lindsey, op. cit., p. 15.

[15]408 U.S. 471 (1972).

[16]Ibid., 490.

[17]See also *Hyser v. Reed.* 318 F.2d 225, 248 (D.C. Cir.), C. J. Bazelon concurring and dissenting, *cert. denied,* 375 U.S. 957 (1963).

[18]408 U.S. at 483.

[19]Ibid., 489. The court suggested that fewer safeguards should be required "in making a prediction as to the ability of the individual to live in society without committing antisocial acts" than in deciding a "wholly retrospective factual question." Id. at 480, 479. For a critical analysis of this approach, see Dershowitz, "Preventive Confinement," 1277.

[20]8 Cal. 3d 410, 503 P.2d 921, 105 Cal. Rptr. 217 (1972).

[21]Ibid., 438, 503 P.2d at 940, 105 Cal. Rptr. at 236. Lynch also challenged his confinement on the familiar ground that the repeated denial of his parole was based on his refusal to confess to having committed additional acts of indecent exposure. Id. at 438 n.26, 503 P.2d at 940 n.26, 105 Cal. Rptr. at 236n. 26. The court did not reach that issue.

[22]Ibid., 415, 503 P.2d at 923, 105 Cal. Rptr. at 219.

[23]Ibid., 438, 503 P.2d at 940, 105 Cal. Rptr. at 236.

[24]Ibid., 421, 503 P.2d at 928, 105 Cal. Rptr. at 224.

[25]The court cited a series of ambiguous Supreme Court decisions including *Furman v. Georgia,* 408 U.S. 238 (1972), and a number of decisions directly on point from several states (some of which have constitutional provisions expressly requiring that criminal penalties must be proportioned to the offense). 8 Cal. 3d at 422–423, 503 P.2d at 928–929, 105, Cal. Rptr. at 224–225. See also *Watson v. United States,* 439 F.2d 442, 464 (D.C. Cir. 1970), appended opinion of Chief Judge Bazelon, subsequently vacated en banc.

[26]8 Cal. 3d at 424, 503 P.2d at 930, 105 Cal. Rptr. at 226.

[27]Ibid., 425, 503 P.2d at 930, 105 Cal. Rptr. at 226.

[28]8 Cal. 3d at 426, 503 P.2d at 931, 105 Cal. Rptr. at 227.

[29]Ibid., 427, 503 P.2d at 932, 105 Cal. Rptr. at 228.

[30]California Health and Safety Code §11352 (formerly §11501).

[31]*In re Foss,* 10 Cal. 3d 910, 112 Cal. Rptr. 649, 519 P.2d 1073 (1974).

[32]*In re Foss, supra,* 10 Cal. 3d 910, 919, 112 Cal. rptr. 649, 654, 519, P.2d 1073, 1078.

[33]Ibid., 929, 112 Cal. Rptr. at 661, 519 P.2d at 1097.

[34]*People v. Wingo,*—Cal. 3d.—,121 Cal. Rptr. 97, 534 P.2d 1001 (1975), and *In re Rodriguez,*—Cal. 3d—, 122 Cal. Rptr. 552, 537 P.2d 384 (1975).

[35]California Penal Code §245(a).

[36]Cal. 3d—, 122 Cal. Rptr. 552, 537 P.2d 384 (1975).

[37]California Penal Code 288: "Any person who shall willfully and lewdly commit any lewd or lascivious act including any of the acts constituting other crimes provided for in part one of this code upon or with the body, or any part or member thereof, of a child under the age of fourteen years, with the intent of arousing, appealing to, or gratifying the lust or passions or sexual desires of such person or of such child, shall be guilty of a felony and shall be imprisoned in the State prison for a term of from one year to life."

[38]The court noted other mitigating factors including the lack of force or weapons, the petitioner's age—22—at the time of the offense, his limited intelligence, and his problems coping with sexual inadequacy.

## Chapter VII

[1]S. Rubin, "The Indeterminate Sentence—Success or Failure?" *National Probation and Parole Association Focus* (March 1949), p. 47; Rubin, "Long Prison Terms and the Form of Sentence," *National Probation and Parole Association Journal,* 2 (1956):337, 344–347. See also P. Tappan, "Sentencing under the Model Penal Code," *Law and Contemporary Problems,* 23 (1958):528, 531: "Another [consequence of the indeterminate sentence and parole] has been the establishment in certain jurisdictions of what seems unnecessarily high permissible terms. . . ."

[2]C. C. Van Vechten, "The Parole Violation Rate," *Journal of Criminal Law and Criminology,* 27 (1937):638.

[3]Rubin, op. cit., p. 347.

[4]Tappan, op. cit., pp. 532, 535. Presumably, higher sentences in a high-crime jurisdiction reflect an effort to deter crime in response to the high rate. Another factor cited is that 13 of the 18 definite-sentence jurisdictions are southern states; this region traditionally has employed a policy of low sentences, except in special cases.

These factors, however, cannot explain intrastate sentence-duration disparities, such as existed in Connecticut until 1968. A statute there permitted the possibility of certain women offenders on indeterminate terms being subject to maximum sentences longer than those that could be given to men serving relatively determinate terms for the identical offenses. Two 1968 cases invalidated the scheme. *United States ex rel. Robinson v. York,* 281 F.Supp 8 (D. Conn. 1968); *Liberti v. York,* 28 Conn Supp. 9, 246 A.2d 106 (Sup. Ct. 1968).

Laws in Pennsylvania and New Jersey until recently required many women to receive indeterminate sentences with the maximum set at the maximum allowed for the crime, while men could receive shorter minimum-maximum terms at the discretion of the judge. The laws were invalidated on equal-protection grounds. *Commonwealth v. Daniel,* 430 Pa. 642, 243 A.2d 400 (1968); *State v. Chambers,* 63 N.J. 287, 307 A.2d 78 (1973). The sentencing schemes did not necessarily mean that women served longer sentences than men, although a study has indicated that mandatory indeterminate terms usually do result in female offenders serving more time than their male counterparts; see Comment, "Sex and Sentencing," *Southwestern Law Journal,* 26 (1972):890. At the very least the Pennsylvania and New Jersey statutes made women subject for reincarceration for parole violations for a longer period than most men; see 430 Pa. at 647 n.*, 243 A.2d at 402–403 n.6. The Supreme Court of New Jersey characterized the rationale of the statutes as follows: ". . . that females are better subjects for rehabilitation, thereby justifying a potentially longer period of detention for that purpose. . . ." 63 N.J. at 296, 307, A.2d at 82.